THE WORKS

PAUL COOKSON

Paul Cookson is one of the busiest poets around. He spends most of his time visiting schools throughout the country performing his work and encouraging others to write their own poems. He has visited well over a thousand schools.

He regularly appears at literature festivals and has been involved with countless In Service Training courses for teachers and librarians.

In addition to this he has edited a number of very successful poetry anthologies, as well as having several of his own collections published. His poems also feature in numerous other anthologies.

A fully qualified teacher, Paul worked full-time for five years. Since 1989 he has taught part-time and now he teaches Drama one day a week in a Nottinghamshire secondary school.

Occasionally he has time to write his own poems.

Paul regularly works with the poet David Harmer. Together they are *Spill The Beans* – a highly original and successful performance poetry double act.

Paul lives in Retford with his wife Sally and two children, Sam and Daisy.

If he does have any spare time he likes to play five-a-side football, listen to his Slade records, read Stephen King books and eat Chinese food while checking ceefax for Everton's results and watching *The Grimleys* . . . often at the same time.

"Paul Cookson is a supreme tickler of funny bones" David Orme

"Sparkling poems full of humour from a very popular performance poet" John Foster

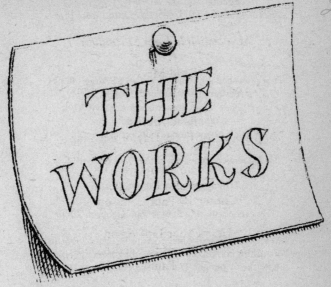

Poems chosen by
Paul Cookson

MACMILLAN CHILDREN'S BOOKS

Dedicated to Daisy and Sam
(Special thanks to Sally, Gaby,
Peter and Rosie Donnelly, David and Pie)

First published 2000 by Macmillan Children's Books
a division of Macmillan Publishers Ltd
20 New Wharf Road, London N1 9RR
Basingstoke and Oxford
www.panmacmillan.com

Associated companies throughout the world

ISBN 0 330 48104 5

15 17 19 18 16

A CIP catalogue record for this book is available from the British Library.

Typeset by SX Composing DTP, Rayleigh, Essex
Printed and bound in Great Britain by Mackays of Chatham plc, Kent

Contents

Contents

Contents

Modern Rhymes

Traditional Stories in Simple Rhyme

Fables and Parables

Contents

Myths and Legends

Humorous Verse

Tongue Twisters

Contents

Puns and Wordplay

Shape Poems/Calligrams/Concrete Verse

Contents

Acrostic Poems

Thin Poems

Poems About the Senses

Contents

Modern Poems

Contents

Contents

Kennings

Riddles

Contents

Limericks

Clerihews

Lists

Contents

Contents

Epitaphs

Elegies

Nonsense Poems

Contents

Adverts/Jingles

Letters

Contents

Diaries

Couplets

Songs

Contents

Performance Poems

Raps

Contents

Choral Poems

Narrative Poems

Conversations and Monologues

Contents

Classic Poems

Contents

The Works – Foreword

This collection provides a lively spread of poetry that covers just about any aspect you could wish for. It's a bumper book for children – and adults – to dip into. It addresses the range of poetry outlined in the National Literacy Strategy so that it makes a useful resource for teachers as well as children. There is a balance of poems that are selected just for the sheer fun, poems that are there for the pleasure of sounds in words – and there are poems that are there to puzzle and intrigue. You will find classic poems rubbing shoulders with playground rhymes. Plus poems from around the world – and some from just down the road.

Poets do not live in ivory towers any more (and they probably never did). They are like you and me. This book shows the range of what we might happily call 'poetry'. Some of it is what my dad used to call, 'plain daft'. And in a way much poetry is daft – look at a simile. 'My love is like a red rose' – well, what could be dafter than that?! Poetry has its roots in play. Early playground rhymes are often based upon in-vented, silly words and rhymes – but somehow they are extremely memorable. Many have lasted for centuries. A rhyme such as –

> 'Inky pinky ponky,
> my daddy saw a donkey,

the donkey died,
daddy cried,
inky pinky ponky'

may raise a laugh. It certainly is daft. But those few frail words have lasted many years, handed down the line by children. For there is a magic within the sounds and the silliness that speaks straight to a vital part of our lives – the part that revels in fun.

But this book takes in all aspects of our lives – the many different voices and ideas show the full range of human experience. For poetry is a way of capturing and recreating our lives – this is what happened and this is how I saw it – the poet shaping words like a diamond cutter, till the poem is perfect and sparks its own brilliance. Poetry is a way of explaining the world to ourselves and ourselves to the world. It can capture our excitement, our imaginings, our wonder, our sadness – and explain feelings that we hardly knew were there. So, some of the poems are serious, sitting happily alongside the more playful. Some of the poems you may not understand – but read the words aloud and listen to the way the sounds run together creating a power of their own. Not everything in life is easy to follow. Why do magnets attract, how can a cloud hold a storm, why should a heart beat? Much is a mystery – but that does not stop us from standing in the summer rain, with our faces turned upward, enjoying the feel of fresh water. So, bathe in the sound of the words. For in the end poetry is a serious game. Step inside this book – and play.

Pie Corbett. April 2000.

Nursery/ Traditional Rhymes

Rhymes and verses that have been passed down from generation to generation so some of them are now very old.

Daddy's Gone to Market

Daddy's gone to market
Mummy's gone to sea
Brother's eating sausages
One, two, three.

Valerie Bloom

Granny's in the Kitchen

Granny's in the kitchen,
Making bread and tea,
There's a monkey in the shed,
But he can't catch me.

Valerie Bloom

Fishes in the River

Fishes in the river,
Fishes in the sea,
Fishes in the saucepan,
Fishes for my tea.

Valerie Bloom

A-gallop, A-gallop, A-gallop

A-gallop, a-gallop, a-gallop,
Off to the sea we go,
A-gallop, a-gallop, a-gallop,
Look at the sands below,
A-gallop, a-gallop, a-gallop,
Oh, it's starting to rain!
A-gallop, a-gallop, a-gallop,
We gallop home again.

Valerie Bloom

Little Jack Horner

Little Jack Horner
Sat in the corner,
Eating a Christmas pie;
He put in his thumb,
And pulled out a plum,
And said, What a good boy am I!

Anon.

Jack and Jill

Jack and Jill went up the hill,
    To fetch a pail of water;
Jack fell down, and broke his crown,
    And Jill came tumbling after.

Anon.

Humpty Dumpty

Humpty Dumpty sat on a wall,
Humpty Dumpty had a great fall;
    All the king's horses,
    And all the king's men,
Couldn't put Humpty together again.

Anon.

The Grand Old Duke of York

The Grand Old Duke of York,
He had ten thousand men,
He marched them up to the top of the hill,
And he marched them down again.
And when they were up they were up,
And when they were down they were down,
And when they were only halfway up
They were neither up nor down.

Anon.

Hey Diddle Diddle

Hey diddle diddle,
The cat and the fiddle,
The cow jumped over the moon;
The little dog laughed
To see such sport,
And the dish ran away
With the spoon.

Anon.

Three Blind Mice

Three blind mice, see how they run!
They all ran after the farmer's wife,
Who cut off their tails with a carving knife,
Did you ever see such a thing in your life
As three blind mice?

Anon.

Little Miss Muffet

Little Miss Muffet
Sat on a tuffet,
Eating her curds and whey;
There came a big spider,
Who sat down beside her
And frightened Miss Muffet away.

Anon.

Old Mother Hubbard

Old Mother Hubbard,
She went to the cupboard
To fetch her poor dog a bone,
But when she got there,
The cupboard was bare,
And so the poor dog had none.

Anon.

Wee Willie Winkie

Wee Willie Winkie
Runs through the town,
Upstairs and downstairs
In his night-gown,
Rapping at the window,
Crying through the lock,
Are the children all in bed,
For now it's eight o'clock?

Anon.

Jack Be Nimble

Jack be nimble,
Jack be quick,
Jack jump over
The candlestick.

Anon.

Diddle Diddle Dumpling, My Son John

Diddle diddle dumpling, my son John,
Went to bed with his breeches on,
One shoe off and one shoe on;
Diddle diddle dumpling, my son John.

Anon.

Twinkle, Twinkle, Little Star

Twinkle, twinkle, little star,
How I wonder what you are!
Up above the world so high,
Like a diamond in the sky!

When the blazing sun is gone,
When he nothing shines upon,
Then you show your little light,
Twinkle, twinkle, all the night.

Anon.

Little Betty Blue

Little Betty Blue
Lost her holiday shoe,
What can little Betty do?
Give her another
To match the other,
And then she may walk out in two.

Anon.

See-saw, Margery Daw

See-saw, Margery Daw,
Sold her bed and lay upon straw,
Sold the straw and lay upon grass
To buy herself a looking-glass.

Anon.

Lucy Locket

Lucy Locket lost her pocket,
Kitty Fisher found it;
Not a penny was there in it,
Only ribbon round it.

Anon.

There was a Little Girl

There was a little girl, and she had a little curl
  Right in the middle of her forehead;
When she was good she was very, very good,
  But when she was bad she was horrid.

Anon.

Little Girls

What are little girls made of?
Sugar and spice
And all things nice
That's what little girls are made of.

Anon.

Little Boys

What are little boys made of?
Frogs and snails
And puppy-dogs' tails
That's what little boys are made of.

Anon.

Georgie Porgie

Georgie Porgie, pudding and pie,
Kissed the girls and made them cry;
When the boys came out to play,
Georgie Porgie ran away.

Anon.

Andy Pandy

Andy Pandy, fine and dandy,
Loves plum cake and sugar candy.
Bought it from a candy shop
And away did hop, hop, hop.

Anon.

Action Verses

Simple poems with predictable structures and rhymes
that have actions to accompany them.

One, Two, Buckle My Shoe

One, two,
Buckle my shoe;

Three, four,
Knock at the door;

Five, six,
Pick up sticks;

Seven, eight,
Lay them straight;

Nine, ten,
A big fat hen;

Eleven, twelve,
Dig and delve;

Thirteen, fourteen,
Maids a-courting;

Fifteen, sixteen,
Maids in the kitchen;

Seventeen, eighteen,
Maids in waiting;

Nineteen, twenty,
My plate's empty.

Anon.

Ring-a-Ring o' Roses

Children hold hands and skip round in a ring.
On the last line of each verse they all sit down on the
ground.

Ring-a-ring o' roses,
A pocket full of posies.
  A-tishoo! A-tishoo!
We all fall down.

Ring-a-ring o' roses,
A pocket full of posies.
One for you, and one for me,
And one for little Moses.
A-tishoo! A-tishoo! We all fall down.

Anon.

Two Little Dicky Birds

Two little dicky birds
Sitting on a wall,

Use your two index fingers to be Peter and Paul.

One named Peter.

Wiggle the finger which is Peter.

One named Paul.

Wiggle the finger which is Paul.

Fly away Peter,

Put the finger which is Peter behind your back.

Fly away Paul;

Put the finger which is Paul behind your back.

Come back Peter.
Come back Paul.

Bring each finger back in front of you.

Anon.

Incey Wincey Spider

Incey Wincey spider
Climbing up the spout;

Use all your fingers to show how the spider climbs up.

Down came the rain
And washed the spider out:

Wriggle your fingers down to show the rain.

Out came the sun
And dried up all the rain;

Sweep your hands up and bring them out and down.

Incey Wincey spider
Climbing up again.

Do the same as for the first line.

Anon.

The Morning Rush

Into the bathroom,
Turn on the tap.
Wash away the sleepiness –
Splish! Splosh! Splash!

Into the bedroom,
Pull on your vest.
Quickly! Quickly!
Get yourself dressed.

Down to the kitchen.
No time to lose.
Gobble up your breakfast.
Put on your shoes.

Back to the bathroom.
Squeeze out the paste.
Brush, brush, brush your teeth.
No time to waste.

Look in the mirror.
Comb your hair.
Hurry, scurry, hurry, scurry
Down the stairs.

Pick your school bag
Up off the floor.
Grab your coat
And out through the door.

John Foster

See Me Walking

See me walking down the street,
Can you walk with me?
Walking with my head held high
As proud as can be.

See me skipping down the street,
Can you skip like this?
Throw your head back, look up high
And blow the sun a kiss.

See me jumping down the street,
Jumping oh so high.
Jump like me and stretch your arms
And try to touch the sky.

See me tip-toe down the street,
Softly on the ground.
Tip-toe tip-toe just like me,
Making not a sound.

See me hopping down the street,
Hoppety hoppety hop.
Hop with me until we're tired
And then we'll have to stop.

Clive Webster

Butterfly Inside

	Actions
Caterpillar long	(*Stand up*)
Caterpillar thin	(*Arms straight by side*)
Caterpillar eat	(*Eating action*)
Caterpillar spin	(*Spin round*)
Caterpillar hush	(*Finger to lips*)
Caterpillar hide	(*Hands over face*)
Caterpillar gone	(*Open empty hands*)
Butterfly inside!	(*Join thumbs to 'fly' hands*)

Coral Rumble

Here is the Seed

Here is the seed
Small and round
Hidden underneath
The ground.

Here is the shoot,
Tiny and small,
Slowly slowly
Growing tall.

Here is the sun.
Here is the shower.
Here are the petals.
Here is the flower.

John Foster

Spring Cleaning

(*with actions!*)

Time to clean the windows,
Time to sweep the floors,
Time to roll the rugs up
And beat them out of doors!
Time to wash the curtains
And dust a shelf or two,
Time to shake the duster,
With an A–A–TCHOO!

Sue Cowling

Leap Like a Leopard

Leap like a leopard.
Hop like a kangaroo.
Swing from branch to branch
Like a monkey in a zoo.

Dive like a dolphin.
Plunge like a whale.
Creep like a caterpillar.
Crawl like a snail.

Scuttle like a spider.
Slither like a snake.
Slide like a duck
On a frozen lake.

Skip like a lamb.
Jump like a frog.
Stalk like a cat.
Scamper like a dog.

Plod like an elephant.
Prowl like a bear.
Shuffle like a tortoise.
Sprint like a hare.

Strut like a peacock
With feathers held high.
Glide like an eagle –
The lord of the sky.

John Foster

Chants

Poems written to be chanted out rhythmically by one or more voices, often used for skipping, clapping and ball-bouncing games.

Round and Round

Round and round the playground,
Marching in a line,
I'll hold your hand.
You hold mine.

Round and round the playground
Skipping in a ring
Everybody loves it
When we all sing.

Round and round the playground
That's what we like:
Climbing on the climbing frame,
Riding on the bike.

Round and round the playground,
All together friends.
We're sad, sad, sad
When the school day ends.

John Kitching

We Want to Wear Our Wellies

We want to wear our wellies
When it's windy.
We want to wear our wellies
When it's wet.
We want to wear our wellies
When the weather on the telly
Says it's going to be
The warmest day yet.

We want to wear our wellies
Even though our feet get smelly.
We want to wear our wellies
Because they're *red*.
We want to wear our wellies
When it's wet or warm or windy –
But we *never* wear our wellies in bed!

Dave Ward

The Poetry United Chant

WHAT DO WE WANT		clap clap clap
WHAT DO WE LIKE		clap clap clap
WHAT DO WE LOVE		clap clap clap
GIVE US A	P	clap clap clap
GIVE US AN	O	clap clap clap
GIVE US AN	E	clap clap clap
GIVE US A	T	clap clap clap
GIVE US AN	R	clap clap clap
GIVE US A	Y	clap clap clap

GIVE US THE RHYTHM . . . P O E T R Y
WHAT WE WANT IS POETRY

clap clap clap
clap clap clap
clap clap clap
YES!

Les Baynton

Skip

One skip
Two skip
Three skip
Four.

Five skip
Six skip
Seven skip
More.

Eight skip
Nine skip
Ten skip
Hop.

Skip skip
skip skip
skip skip
STOP.

Andrew Collett

Skipping Rhyme

Cheese
cheese
cheese and bread
cheese and bread
cheese and bread and pickle
cheese and bread and pickle spread
                  spread
                  spread
           pickle spread
cheese and bread and pickle spread
        bread
        bread
cheese and bread
cheese and bread
cheese
cheese
cheese

   and

        PICKLED ONION
        PLEASE!

Judith Nicholls

Summer

Apple – dapple summer
apple – dapple time
poppies red as ribbons
daisies white as lime.
Apples, plums and peaches
songbirds in the trees
summer suns are glowing
picnics
ices
teas.

Apple – dapple summer
pollen in the breeze
thistles pricking fingers
nettles on the knees.
Noses sore with sneezes
eyes as red as wine
summer suns are glowing
and it's called
Ahhhhh Tiiiiiisuuuueeee
time.

Peter Dixon

The Bug Chant

Red bugs, bed bugs,
find them on your head bugs.

Green bugs, mean bugs,
lanky, long and lean bugs.

Pink bugs, sink bugs,
swimming in your drink bugs.

Yellow bugs, mellow bugs,
lazy little fellow bugs.

White bugs, night bugs,
buzzing round the light bugs.

Black bugs, slack bugs,
climbing up your back bugs.

Blue bugs, goo bugs,
find them in your shoe bugs.

Thin bugs, fat bugs,
hiding in your hat bugs.

Big bugs, small bugs,
crawling on your wall bugs.

Smooth bugs, hairy bugs,
flying like a fairy bugs.

Garden bugs, house bugs,
lumpy little louse bugs.

Fierce bugs, tame bugs,
some without a name bugs.

Far bugs, near bugs,
'What's this over here?' bugs.

Whine bugs, drone bugs,
write some of your own bugs.

Bzzzzzzzzzzzzzzzz . . .

Tony Mitton

The Skipping Rope Queen

I never slide and never slip
I never tumble, never trip.
I never tangle, never fall,
I never get tied up at all.
I am the fastest ever seen
I am the playtime skipping queen.

Paul Cookson

Playground Song

Round and round the roundabouts
Fast and slow
Sliding down the slides
High to low
Swinging on the swings
To and fro
Playing in the playground
Watch me go!

Paul Cookson

Underneath the Apple Tree

Two people swing the rope and everyone takes it in turns to find out their future.

The skipper skips until she trips on a letter. Then the others choose a boy's name beginning with that letter. The skipper skips on to discover if they will marry. If the answer is YES, she carries on to find out what she will wear, and so on.

Underneath the apple tree
A boy said to me –
Kiss me, cuddle me,
Who should it be?
A–B–C–D . . .

Will you get married?
Yes, No, Yes, No, . . .

What will he marry you in?
Silk, satin, cotton, rags, . . .

How will you go to your wedding?
Coach, carriage, wheelbarrow, car, . . .

How many children?
1, 2, 3, 4, 5, . . .

Anon.

Lemon Pie, Apple Tart

Skip this game to find out who you will marry!

Lemon pie, apple tart,
Tell me the name of your sweetheart.
A-B-C-D-E-F . . .

Felix is your love,
White doves up above,
Sitting on his knee,
Kissing 1, 2, 3, 4, . . .

Anon.

One, Two, Three, Four, Five

One, two, three, four, five,
Once I caught a fish alive,
Six, seven, eight, nine, ten,
Then I let it go again.
Why did you let it go?
Because it bit my finger so.
Which finger did it bite?
This little finger on the right.

Anon.

Dance to Your Daddy

Dance to your daddy,
My little babby,
Dance to your daddy,
My little lamb;

You shall have a fishy
In a little dishy,
You shall have a fishy
When the boat comes in.

Baby shall have an apple,
Baby shall have a plum,
Baby shall have a rattle
When Daddy comes home.

Anon.

Pat-a-Cake

A clapping rhyme to play with a baby.

Pat-a-cake, pat-a-cake, baker's man,
Bake me a cake as fast as you can;
Pat it and prick it, and mark it with B,
Put it in the oven for Baby and me.

Anon.

Fruits

Half a pawpaw in the basket –
Only one o' we can have it.
Wonder which one that will be?
I have a feeling that is me.

One guinep in the tree
Hanging down there tempting me.
It don' mek no sense to pick it,
One guinep can't feed a cricket.

Two ripe guava pon the shelf,
I know I hid them there meself.
When night com an' it get dark
Me an' them will have a talk.

Three sweet-sop, well I jus' might
Give on o' them a nice big bite.
Cover up the bite jus' so, sis,
Then no one will ever notice.

Four red apple near me chair –
Who so careless put them there?
Them don' know how me love apple?
Well, thank God fer silly people.

Five jew-plum, I can't believe it!
How they know jew-plum's me fav'rit?
But why they hide them in a cupboard?
Cho, people can be so awkward.

Six naseberry, you want a nibble?
Why baby must always dribble?
Come wipe you mout', it don't mek sense
To broadcast the evidence.

Seven mango! What a find!
The smaddy who lef them really kind.
One fe you an' six fe me,
If you want more, climb the tree.

Eight orange fe cousin Clem,
But I have just one problem –
How to get rid o' the eight skin
That the orange them come in.

Nine jackfruit! Not even me
Can finish nine, but let me see,
I don't suppose that they will miss one.
That was hard, but now me done.

Ten banana, mek them stay,
I feeling really full today.
Mek me lie down on me bed, quick.
Lawd, ah feeling really sick.

Valerie Bloom

Modern Rhymes

Simple verses with predictable structures and rhymes.

Song of the Kite

I'm a
space-hopping,
flip-and-flopping,
dipping, diving kite!

Up-and-over,
looming, zooming . . .
Race me through the night!

Blow me,
throw me,
on my windy way!
Dipping, diving,
looming, zooming . . .
Chase me through the day!

Judith Nicholls

The Seaside

Are we nearly there?
Can you see the sea?
Who will be ready first?
Me! me! me!

Does the sand tickle?
Down by the sea
Who can make footprints?
Me! me! me!

The seagulls are crying,
'Shush,' says the sea.
Who dares put a toe in?
Me! me! me!

Jo Peters

The Yo-yo Man

There's a man I know
Who roams the land
With a bright red yo-yo
In his hand!
He twirls it here,
He twirls it there,
He twirls that yo-yo
Everywhere!
He spins it up,
He spins it down,
He spins it all
Around the town!
He whirls his yo-yo
Low and high,
Until it nearly
Hits the sky!
He whips it
Round and round his head,
He even whizzes it
In bed!
And when he slides
Beneath the sheet,
He even yo-yos
In his sleep!

Anne Logan

One for the Cluck of an Angry Hen

One for the cluck of an angry hen.
Two for the cheeps of a tiny wren.
Three for the croak of a fat green frog.
Four for the bark of a jumping dog.
Five for the quack of a duck on a lake.
Six for the hiss of a wriggling snake.
Seven for the hoot of the old grey owl.
Eight for the snarl of a wolf on the prowl.
Nine for the squeak of a scuttling rat.
Ten for the purr of a snuggling cat.

John Foster

B, Beautiful B!

I'm a
busy, buzzing,
black and yellow bumble-bee.
Bzzz, bzzz, bzzz,
you can't catch me!

I'm a
bobbing, bouncing,
belly-dancing butterfly.
Bib, bab, bob,
watch me reach the sky!

I'm a
bossy, bungling,
bumpy-jumpy big brown bear.
Oomps-a-daisy, bumps-a-daisy,
chase me if you dare!

Judith Nicholls

The Caterpillar Fair

Ten little caterpillars
wriggled to the fair.
What did they do
when they got there?

One ate potatoes,
one ate pie,
one bought a telescope
to look at the sky.

One blew a trumpet,
one played guitar,
two sat together
in a dodgem car.

One met an elephant,
one saw a seal
and one went riding
on the whirly whirly wheel!

Irene Rawnsley

Run, Run!

Run, run –
Here comes Mum,
She's got porridge in her hair.

Run, run –
Here comes Mum,
She's found the spider on her chair.

Run, run –
Here comes Mum,
And she knows who put it there!

Dave Ward

Penguins on Ice

Every penguin's mum
can toboggan on her tum.
She can only do that
as she's fluffy and fat:

> *It must be nice*
> *to live on ice.*

Every penguin's dad
is happy and glad.
He can slip and slide
and swim and glide:

> *It must be nice*
> *to live on ice.*

All penguin chicks
do slippery tricks.
They waddle and fall
but don't mind at all:

> *It must be nice*
> *to live on ice.*

Celia Warren

Dinner Lady

Today at school
I cut my knee.
The dinner lady
looked after me.

She washed away
the blood and dirt,
then put a plaster
where it hurt.

David Harmer

Down the River

I got in my boat and went down the river,
the full, flowing river,
the river that goes through the jungle.

I paddled my boat down the river,
the waving, winding river,
the river that goes through the jungle.

I saw lots of wonders in that river,
    golden plants and golden flowers,
    a dead croc with a sword in it,
    a square box of diamonds,
    a starfish bigger than me,
    a diver looking for treasure,
    a machine-gun and a water-pistol,
    a big, golden teapot –

All these were in the river, and on the river
    was a ladder floating,
    a red, pink and orange rock,
    another, much bigger boat
    half-sticking out of the water,
    a swimming costume that fitted,
    a skipping rope I sprayed
    till it shone with gold,
    a sign saying *Danger: Waterfall*.

I stuck to my boat in the river,
    the up and down river,
    the flooding, floating river.

I saw dangers around the river,
    a house that was alive
    and was trying to catch me,
    a dead bird falling down,
    black bumble-bees flying
    and landing on a shot boy,
    a tail moving and a glimpse of eyes.

I kept on paddling down the river,
  the full, flowing river,
  the waving, winding river.

I saw an enormous diamond in the river,
  pink, green, orange and blue,
  colours changing in the sun.
  I stopped my boat by it,
  it was smooth and felt like china.
  I didn't want to climb on it,
  but some of the diamond fell off
  and I brought it home.

Home in my boat, down the river,
  the up and down river,
  the river that goes through the jungle.

Matthew Sweeney

Written with the 1990 reception class of Aylward First and Middle School, after a performance by Peter Cutts.

Traditional Stories in Simple Rhyme

Traditional stories are stories that have been around for ages and passed down through the ages. Some traditional stories can be thousands of years old.

Little Red Riding Hood and the Wolf

As soon as Wolf began to feel
That he would like a decent meal,
He went and knocked on Grandma's door.
When Grandma opened it, she saw
The sharp white teeth, the horrid grin,
And Wolfie said, 'May I come in?'
Poor Grandmamma was terrified,
'He's going to eat me up!' she cried.
And she was absolutely right.
He ate her up in one big bite.
But Grandmamma was small and tough,
And Wolfie wailed, 'That's not enough!
I haven't yet begun to feel
That I have had a decent meal!'
He ran around the kitchen yelping,
'I've *got* to have another helping!'
Then added with a frightful leer,
'I'm therefore going to wait right here
Till Little Miss Red Riding Hood
Comes home from walking in the wood.'
He quickly put on Grandma's clothes,
(Of course he hadn't eaten those.)
He dressed himself in coat and hat.
He put on shoes and after that
He even brushed and curled his hair,
Then sat himself in Grandma's chair.
In came the little girl in red.
She stopped. She stared. And then she said,

'*What great big ears you have, Grandma.*'
'*All the better to hear you with,*' the Wolf replied.
'*What great big eyes you have, Grandma,*'
    said Little Red Riding Hood.
'*All the better to see you with,*' the Wolf replied.
He sat there watching her and smiled.
He thought, I'm going to eat this child.
Compared with her old Grandmamma
She's going to taste like caviare.
Then Little Red Riding Hood said, '*But Grandma,*
what a lovely great big furry coat you have on.'
'That's wrong!' cried Wolf. 'Have you forgot
To tell me what BIG TEETH I've got?
Ah well, no matter what you say,
I'm going to eat you anyway.'
The small girl smiles. One eyelid flickers.
She whips a pistol from her knickers.
She aims it at the creature's head
And *bang bang bang*, she shoots him dead.
A few weeks later, in the wood,
I came across Miss Riding Hood.
But what a change! No cloak of red,
No silly hood upon her head.
She said, 'Hello, and do please note
My lovely furry WOLFSKIN COAT.'

Roald Dahl

How the Tortoise Got Its Shell

Come to my feast!
cried the great god Zeus.
Today I shall be wed!
And from each corner of the earth
all Zeus's creatures sped . . .

The fliers and the creepers,
the long, the short, the tall;
the crawlers and the leapers,
the feathered, furred and bald;
hunters, biters, finders, fighters,
hooters, whistlers, roarers;
squeakers, screamers, squawkers, dreamers,
nibblers, gulpers, borers.
Paws and claws from hills and shores
from south, from north, from west and east,
from mountain tops and forest floors
all Zeus's creatures joined the feast
except
                                  the tortoise.

They raved, they pranced, they feasted, danced;
six days and nights each creature stayed
to chatter, flatter, clap and cheer
at the great god Zeus's grand parade
except
                                  the tortoise.

Next day . . .
Why weren't you there, my friend, asked Zeus,
the day that I was wed?

The tortoise smiled her small, slow smile
and raised her small, slow head.

A wedding feast is fun, I guess,
but I'm a simple one.
I'm happy by myself, she said.
There's no place quite like home!

How dare you stay away! roared Zeus.
I'll show you just what for!
From this day on you'll carry your home
on your back, for evermore!

Judith Nicholls

The Three Little Pigs

The first little pig in a house of straw
heard a tap tap tap on her little green door.
'Little pig, little pig, let me come in,'
said the big bad wolf with a big bad grin.
Then he huffed and he puffed and he huffed some more
and down went the little pig's house of straw.
The next little pig was taking a nap
in her house of sticks when she heard a tap
and the big bad wolf with a big bad grin
gave a huff and a puff and blew her house in.
Then the big bad wolf, still up to his tricks
went off to the third little house of bricks.
'Little pig, little pig, let me come in,'
said the big bad wolf with a big bad grin.
And he huffed and he puffed till his face turned red.
'My house is too tough,' the little pig said.
'I'll come down the chimney,' the wolf yelled, 'Now!'
But the fire was lit and the wolf yelled 'Ow!'
and shot straight out in a cloud of smoke
as the third little pig gave the fire a poke.
Then the wolf blew on his paws with a huff and a puff
and he hobbled off home. He'd had enough.

Marian Swinger

How the Bumble-Bee Got His Stripes

On the day that the world began,
Each of the creatures was shown
All the colours of the universe;
And all were told to choose
Which of these they wanted for themselves.

Well, that day the elephant
Thought carefully and chose to be grey,
But the bumble-bee
Just bumbled around and buzzed around
And couldn't make up his mind
And the yellow sun shone so brightly
That the bumble-bee's bum became yellow.

And that night the goldfish
Thought carefully and chose to be golden,
But the bumble-bee
Just bumbled around and buzzed around
And couldn't make up his mind,
And the black night grew so dark
That the bumble-bee's hips became black.

And next day the cricket
Thought carefully and chose to be green,
But the bumble-bee
Just bumbled around and buzzed around
And couldn't make up his mind,
And the yellow sun shone so brightly
That the bumble-bee's waist became yellow.

And that night the owl
Thought carefully and chose to be brown,
But the bumble-bee
Just bumbled around and buzzed around
And couldn't make up his mind,
And the black night grew so dark
That the bumble-bee's chest became black.

And next day the polar bear
Thought carefully and chose to be white,
But the bumble-bee
Just bumbled around and buzzed around
And couldn't make up his mind,
And the yellow sun shone so brightly
That the bumble-bee's shoulders became yellow.

And that night the jay
Thought carefully and chose to be blue,
But the bumble-bee
Just bumbled around and buzzed around
And couldn't make up his mind,
And the black night grew so dark
That the bumble-bee's neck and head and legs
  became black.

And next day the bumble-bee
Began to be thoughtful.
He bumbled around and buzzed around
But thought carefully,
And chose the colours he wanted to be.
He said, 'I've made up my mind.
I want to be all the colours of the rainbow.'
But it was too late
Because the bumble-bee
Had already become
Black-striped
And yellow-striped,
From the top of his head
To the tip of his toes.

Nick Toczek

The Farmer's Cat

From the traditional Chinese.

Out in the fields
in spring time,
the farmer's cat follows him
as he plants the seeds of corn.

The cat dances with the raindrops
and sleeps in the sun
and when autumn comes
she sees that the farmer
has a field full of corn.

Out in the fields
in spring time,
the farmer's cat follows him
as he plants the peanut seeds.

The cat dances with the raindrops
and sleeps in the sun
and when autumn comes
she sees that the farmer
has a field of tasty peanuts.

Out in the fields
in spring time,
the farmer watches while his cat
plants rows of tiny fish.

The cat dances with the raindrops
and sleeps in the sun
and dreams that when autumn comes
she will fill her dish
with all the silver fish
that she's grown in the farmer's fields.

David Greygoose

The Owl and the Pussy-Cat

The Owl and the Pussy-Cat went to sea
 In a beautiful pea-green boat,
They took some honey, and plenty of money,
 Wrapped up in a five-pound note.
The Owl looked up to the stars above,
 And sang to a small guitar,
'O lovely Pussy! O Pussy, my love,
 What a beautiful Pussy you are,
  You are,
  You are!
 What a beautiful Pussy you are!'

Pussy said to the Owl, 'You elegant fowl!
  How charmingly sweet you sing!
O let us be married! too long have we tarried:
  But what shall we do for a ring?'
They sailed away, for a year and a day,
  To the land where the Bong-tree grows,
And there in a wood a Piggy-wig stood
  With a ring at the end of his nose,
    His nose,
    His nose,
  With a ring at the end of his nose.

'Dear Pig, are you willing to sell for one shilling
  Your ring?' Said the Piggy, 'I will.'
So they took it away, and were married next day
  By the Turkey who lives on the hill.
They dined on mince, and slices of quince,
  Which they ate with a runcible spoon;
And hand in hand, on the edge of the sand,
  They danced by the light of the moon,
    The moon,
    The moon,
  They danced by the light of the moon.

                              Edward Lear

Fables and Parables

These are stories and poems that have a moral to teach us.

Tortoise and Hare Race

'Tortoise, you're very slow you know.
No wonder. Your legs are so short.'

'I get to where I want to go,'
said Tortoise with a snort.

Hare
was everywhere,
light and springy,
pinging past
fast,
all over the place.

'Besides I'd beat you in a race
if we were having one.'
'All right, we'll let Fox choose the place,
and see it's fairly run.'

The race began.
Off Hare ran.
'I'll probably win
before you begin,'
he jeered
as he disappeared.

And Tortoise *was* slow getting away
but he said as he jogged along,
'Little by little wins the day.
And Hare will get bored before long.'

Hare
was so sure
he'd be there
before
the Tortoise,
he thought
he'd take
a short break
and fell deep
asleep
in the sun.

He slept
and slept
while the minutes
kept on ticking away
through the heat of the day.

And still he slept

as Tortoise crept up and passed
on his way to the Finishing Post.
The end of the race was in sight at last.
He expected Hare there to boast.

But Hare woke
with a shock.
His body-clock
said he'd overslept.
So up he leapt
and started to run –
but there was someone
already ahead
and at this minute
about to win.
'It can't be Tortoise.'
But it was.

Yes, there ahead with Fox was Tortoise –
winner of the race
and that despite his legs' shortness
and his slow pace.

Jill Townsend

Bottles

Each of the bottles is filled with water.
This is important to remember.
They may bear different names on the labels.
They may appear to be different colours.
But each of the bottles is filled with water.

They stand in a line on a stall
in the far corner of the market.

The first woman comes,
and buys one of the bottles.
She thinks the bottle contains wine.
She takes it home to drink with her husband.
They end the night tipsy with ecstasy, falling
into each other's arms.

The second woman comes,
and buys the second bottle.
She thinks the bottle contains perfume.
She takes it home and sprinkles it
on her arms and on her neck.
She smiles at the men who smile at her,
thinking they can smell the scent
that she cannot smell.

The third woman comes,
and buys the third bottle.
She thinks the bottle contains medicine.
She takes it home and gives a spoonful
to each of her sick children.
The next day their eyes are laughing
as they sing and play in the street.

The fourth woman comes,
and asks for water.
The stall-keeper shrugs and points at the labels.
The woman unscrews the largest bottle, the one
with the water dyed the most exotic colour,
the one with the highest price on the label.

'I'll take this one,' she says, and stands
where she is and drinks every drop.
The stall-keeper, brazen-faced, still asks
for his money.
The woman bends down and picks up a stone.
'Here is a loaf of bread,' she says.

Dave Ward

The Lion and the Mouse

Beneath the spreading baobab,
the lion slept.

Mouse scuttled over parched earth,
climbed unwittingly the sandy mound
then saw – too late.
Fresh from hungry dreams
the lion woke
and snatched the mouse.

Spare me, free me, please!
begged Mouse.
Oh, wise and strong and tall,
lord of all hunters,
king of all creatures;
your strength and power are great,
my strength is small . . .

Save me, spare my life, I pray!
Though I am weak, I know,
I promise that one day
I will repay you.
Let me go!

The lion roared with mirth.
You, repay me?
You, one of the smallest on the earth . . .?
We'll see!

Yet, shaking still with mirth,
he set him free.

The mouse walked free –
but not the lion.
When next they met
the lion, whimpering in despair,
lay tangled in a hunter's net,
roped to a tree.

At last, my turn!
cried grateful Mouse.
Now I can keep my promise,
just you see!

And patiently he bit and gnawed,
he gnawed and bit until, at last,
the net was opened up:

the lion was free!

Judith Nicholls

The Fox and the Grapes

a fable by Aesop

Grapes are growing, round and ripe,
High upon the vine.
Fox says, as he licks his lips,
'Those grapes will soon be mine.'

The grapes look plump and juicy.
The fox, on his hind legs,
Stretches up to reach for them
Just like a dog that begs.

Fox jumps and keeps on jumping
To try and take his treat.
The grapes will be so tasty:
Succulent and sweet.

At last, the hungry fox gives up.
He's tried for many an hour.
He cannot reach the fruit and cries:
'I bet those grapes are sour!'

MORAL

If something is good,
But it's not to be had,
Don't fool yourself
By pretending it's bad.

Celia Warren

Somewhere in the Sky

Somewhere
In the sky,
There's a door painted blue,
With a big brass knocker seven feet high.
If you can find it,
Knock, and go through –
That is, if you dare.
You'll see behind it
The secrets of the universe piled on a chair
Like a tangle of wool.
A voice will declare
'You have seven centuries in which to unwind it.
But whatever
You do,
You must never,
Ever,
Lose your temper and pull.'

Leo Aylen

Counting the Stars

It's late at night
and John is counting the stars

he's walking through the woods
and counting the stars.

The night is clear
and the stars are like salt

on a black tablecloth.
John counts silently,

his lips moving, his head tilted.
It's late at night

and John is counting the stars
until he walks into a tree

that he never saw
because he was counting the stars.

Look at John
lying in the woods.

The woodland creatures are gathering around him
    laughing.

in little woodland voices.

MORAL: Even when you're looking up,
         Don't forget to look down.

             Ian McMillan

Who is My Neighbour?

From Jerusalem to Jericho
the road was lonely, narrow, slow.

A man came walking down the track
as thieves crept up behind his back.

They knocked him down and beat his head
stripped him, robbed him, left for dead.

He lay there bleeding in the dirt
moaning, groaning, badly hurt.

The sun burned down, his throat ran dry
but then a priest came passing by.

'Water please,' cried out the man.
'Priest, help me any way you can.'

No help came, he was denied
the priest walked by on the other side.

A second priest ignored his plight
just walked away and out of sight.

As a Samaritan drew near
he shouted out in pain and fear,

'My wife and children will grieve for me
I am in the hands of my enemy.'

But with those hands his wounds were bathed
they raised him up and he was saved

Carried as a donkey's load
to an inn along the road.

Washed and bandaged, laid to sleep
two silver coins left for his keep.

'Take care of him,' said his new friend
'I'll pay whatever else you spend

And when he wakes let him know
I was his neighbour not his foe.'

David Harmer

Myths and Legends

These are ancient traditional stories of gods and heroes, tales and happenings and strange occurrences that have often been embellished over the years. Legends are based in distant facts, for example the story of Robin Hood. Myths have been invented to explain why things happen. For example, in Norse mythology every time thunder was heard the god Thor was said to be banging his hammer.

Robin Hood
14th Century

Robin Hood
Was an outlawed earl
He took to the wood
With a lovely girl,
And there and then
They were lord and queen
Of a band of men
In Lincoln green –
There was Scarlet Will, and Alan a Dale,
And great big Little John-O,
And Friar Tuck, that fat old buck,
And Much the Miller's son-0!

Robin Hood
He robbed the rich
And gave to the good
And needy, which,
When the moon was bright
And the sport was rare,
Seemed only right
And fair and square
To Scarlet Will, and Alan a Dale,
And great big Little John-O,
And Friar Tuck, that fat old buck,
And Much the Miller's son-O!

Robin Hood
He poached the deer
And moistened his food
With stolen beer –
Hark how they sing
And shout and flout
The knavish king
Who turned him out
With Scarlet Will, and Alan a Dale,
And great big Little John-O,
And Friar Tuck, that fat old buck,
And Much the Miller's son-O!

Eleanor Farjeon

The Mud Mother

With eyes of mud and a snail's tongue
She dines
On the corpses of otters, water-rats and voles.
Her babies
Suckle mud from the riverbanks.
At night
She orders her brood to crawl up into boats,
And,
From the sleeping crew,
Steal a life or two.
If a river is tinged with red
You can bet
The Mud Mother lives there.
Her hair
Gets mistaken for the long green weeds,
Her voice
For the gurgling of water over stones.

Brian Patten

Egyptian Afterlife

So, Osiris, please tell me
What happens when I die?

First, mortal,
you must persuade the ferryman
to ferry you across
the river of death

And if I manage that?

Then you must pass through
The Twelve Gates
Each guarded
by a ferocious serpent

Twelve gates?
Sounds tricky.
But if I make it?

Your third ordeal will be to cross
The blazing Lake of Fire
Where you will be judged

Oh, I see. And if by chance
I've led a blameless life?

Why, you will live forever
And your soul
Will travel through
The heavens

But what if I have sinned?

Ha! Then you
will be fed to the monster!

Why bother?
Just feed me to the monster now.

Roger Stevens

Thunderbird

The song of Little-Nose, the totem-carver

When the boy Little-Nose asked to become a carver, the adult carvers told him in jest that he could only join them if he carved an image of the Thunderbird (which no person had ever seen in the flesh). Undaunted, Little-Nose set out in his frail canoe and found this great spirit of the weathers. In return for honouring Little-Nose's visit, and for taking him back to his people, the Thunderbird demanded that his image be placed at the top of all Totems. Little-Nose was the first to carve it. (North-American Legend)

I have sought the Thunderbird.
I have sailed far from home.
I have voyaged over the swell
and the wild sea-foam.

I have heard the Thunderbird
as each wide mighty flap
of its wings ripped the air
with the thunderclap.

I have seen the Thunderbird.
I have watched it rise.
I have witnessed the lightning
lance from its eyes.

I have awed at the Thunderbird
hunting up high.
I have gasped as it lifted
a whale to the sky.

I have fronted its face
and its terrible beak.
I have told it my purpose
and heard it speak.

I have ridden its flight.
I have clung to its feathers
as it soared through the clouds
to scatter the weathers.

I have come back to tell
in the place of my birth
how the Thunderbird waters
our Mother Earth.

I have carved the Thunderbird
for all folk to see
up at the top
of the Totem Tree.

Tony Mitton

How Fire Came to Earth

An Aboriginal Legend

In the Dream-Time, at the naming
Of the hills and trees and rivers,
Old Wakala sat in darkness,
Wished he had a fire to sit by,
Saw a blaze up in the heavens
Flashing brightly in the darkness
But the Karak-Karak snatched it,
Seven sisters, spirit-women,
Took it home and did not share it.
When the morning came the sisters
Fetched their bags to go out hunting.
Then Wakala called out to them,
'Come and eat your breakfast with me.
You and I will hunt together.'
After breakfast they went hunting
And Wakala watched the women,
Thinking he would steal their secret.
As they dug for roots and insects
With the pointed sticks they carried
Sparks went flying. Then Wakala
Knew the fire must be inside them.
After supper sly Wakala
Asked a question of the women.
'Sisters, which food is your favourite?'
'We eat most things,' said the sisters,
'Juicy termites are our favourite.

Only snakes are hateful to us.'
Then Wakala lay down, smiling.
Rising early, just as day broke,
He crept off and left them sleeping,
Looked for snakes and caught a bagful,
Found a termites' nest and quickly
Filled it with the writhing creatures.
Then he called the Karak-Karak –
'Come and see what I have found you!'
Seven sisters soon came running,
Saw the nest and tore it open!
Snakes leapt at them, hissing, squirming!
Terrified, the screaming women
Used their digging sticks as weapons,
Striking sparks upon the dry ground.
In an instant bold Wakala
Gathered up the glowing embers,
Ran away and left the sisters.
'Now the fire is mine!' he shouted,
Running, dancing like a madman.
All the snakes lay dead or dying
And the digging sticks were broken.
Then the wailing spirit-women
Felt the cold and could not bear it
So a wind came rushing, caught them
By the hair and whirled them upwards.
Seven shooting stars went flying
Up into eternal darkness.
Meanwhile, back on earth, Wakala
Made a fire and sat beside it.

Soon his neighbours came round begging
'Lend us fire to warm and cheer us.'
'Wah! Wah! Wah!' was all he answered,
'Go away! The fire is mine now.'
Then his neighbours turned against him,
Stoned Wakala, tried to kill him
But he picked up coals and flung them,
Setting clumps of dry grass blazing.
So the neighbours lit their torches,
Took them burning, flaming homeward.
'Wah! Wah! Wah!' complained Wakala,
Jumped into the fire to spite them.
Rising ghostly from the ashes
Came a crow with sooty feathers,
Cawing, calling in the daytime
'Wah! Wah! Wah!' While seven sisters
Shining brightly in the night-time
Tell the story over, over,
How fire came to earth in Dream-Time.

Sue Cowling

Duppy Dance

You walk too-too late at night
duppies make your wrong road the right.
Around you, they rattle strings of bones.
   And duppies dance. Duppies dance.

All along deep-deep dark road
duppies croak like one hidden mighty toad.
You hear scary bells toll.
   And duppies dance. Duppies dance.

Duppies make horses-hooves clop-clop.
Make strange big birds flutter up.
Make you feel skin gone shrivelled.
   And duppies dance. Duppies dance.

Roaring ten bulls like one bull
duppies rip off your clothes in one pull.
Skeletons prance around you.
   And duppies dance. Duppies dance.

James Berry

Duppy = a Caribbean word meaning a ghost

Pegasus

From the blood of Medusa
Pegasus sprang.
His hoof upon heaven
Like melody rang,
His whinny was sweeter
Than Orpheus' lyre,
The wing on his shoulder
Was brighter than fire.

His tail was a fountain,
His nostrils were caves,
His mane and his forelock
Were musical waves,
He neighed like a trumpet,
He cooed like a dove,
He was stronger than terror
And swifter than love.

He could not be captured,
He could not be bought,
His running was rhythm,
His standing was thought;
With one eye on sorrow
And one eye on mirth,
He galloped in heaven
And gambolled on earth.

And only the poet
With wings to his brain
Can mount him and ride him
Without any rein,
The stallion of heaven,
The steed of the skies,
The horse of the singer
Who sings as he flies.

Eleanor Farjeon

Humorous Verse

These poems will make you laugh or smile.

Aliens Stole My Underpants

To understand the ways
of alien beings is hard,
and I've never worked it out
why they landed in my backyard.

And I've always wondered why
on their journey from the stars,
these aliens stole my underpants
and took them back to Mars.

They came on a Monday night
when the weekend wash had been done,
pegged out on the line
to be dried by the morning sun.

Mrs Driver from next door
was a witness at the scene
when aliens snatched my underpants –
I'm glad that they were clean!

It seems they were quite choosy
as nothing else was taken.
Do aliens wear underpants
or were they just mistaken?

I think I have a theory
as to what they wanted them for,
they needed to block off a draught
blowing in through the spacecraft door.

Or maybe some Mars museum
wanted items brought back from space.
Just think, my pair of Y-fronts
displayed in their own glass case.

And on the label beneath
would be written where they got 'em
and how such funny underwear
once covered an Earthling's bottom!

Brian Moses

Where Do All the Teachers Go?

Where do all the teachers go
When it's four o'clock?
Do they live in houses
And do they wash their socks?

Do they wear pyjamas
And do they watch TV?
And do they pick their noses
The same as you and me?

Do they live with other people?
Have they mums and dads?
And were they ever children?
And were they ever bad?

Did they ever, never spell right?
Did they ever makes mistakes?
Were they punished in the corner
If they pinched the chocolate flakes?

Did they ever lose their hymn books?
Did they ever leave their greens?
Did they scribble on the desk tops?
Did they wear old dirty jeans?

I'll follow one back home today
I'll find out what they do
Then I'll put it in a poem
That they can read to you.

Peter Dixon

Ettykett

My mother knew a lot about manners,
   she said you should never slurp;
you should hold your saucer firmly,
   and not clang your teeth on the curp.

My father knew nothing of manners,
   all he could do was slurp;
and when I can't find a rhyming word,
   I set about making them urp.

John Rice

Magic Cat

My mum whilst walking through the door
Spilt some magic on the floor.
Blobs of this
and splots of that
but most of it upon the cat.

Our cat turned magic, straight away
and in the garden went to play
where it grew two massive wings
and flew around in fancy rings.
'Oh look!' cried Mother, pointing high,
'I didn't know our cat could fly.'
Then with a dash of Tibby's tail
she turned my mum into a snail!

So now she lives beneath a stone
and dusts around a different home.
And I'm an ant
and Dad's a mouse
And Tibby's living in our house.

Peter Dixon

Can't Be Bothered to Think of a Title

When they make slouching in the chair
an Olympic sport
I'll be there.

When they give out a cup
for refusing to get up
I'll win it every year.

When they hand out the gold
for sitting by the fire
I'll leave the others in the cold,

and when I'm asked to sign my name
in the Apathetic Hall of Fame
I won't go.

Ian McMillan

Where Teachers Keep Their Pets

Mrs Cox has a fox
nesting in her curly locks.

Mr Spratt's tabby cat
sleeps beneath his bobble hat.

Miss Cahoots has various newts
swimming in her zip-up boots.

Mr Spry has Fred his fly
eating food stains from his tie.

Mrs Groat shows off her stoat
round the collar of her coat.

Mr Spare's got grizzly bears
hiding in his spacious flares.

And . . .

Mrs Vickers has a stick insect called 'Stickers'
. . . but no one's ever seen where she keeps it.

Paul Cookson

Proverb

Don't dance on the alligator back
Until yuh sure him dead,
If yuh sit down underneath bird nest
Then cover up yuh head.

Valerie Bloom

An Interesting Fact About One of My Relatives

My

great great great great
great great great great
great great great great
great great great great
great great great great
great great great great
great great great great

grandad is very old.

Ian McMillan

Tongue Twisters

Poems or phrases that rely on alliteration and are therefore difficult to say fast.

Betty Botter

Betty Botter bought some butter,
But, she said, this butter's bitter;
If I put it in my batter,
It will make my batter bitter,
But a bit of better butter
Will make my batter better.
So she bought a bit of butter
Better than her bitter butter
And she put it in her batter,
And it made her batter better,
So 'twas better Betty Botter
Bought a bit of better butter.

Anon.

Three Little Ghostesses

Three little ghostesses,
Sitting on postesses,
Eating buttered toastesses,
Greasing their fistesses,
Up to the wristesses,
Oh, what beastesses
To make such feastesses!

Anon.

Camilla Caterpillar

Camilla Caterpillar kept a caterpillar killer-cat.
A caterpillar killer categorically she kept.
But alas the caterpillar killer-cat attacked Camilla
As Camilla Caterpillar catastrophically slept.

Mike Jubb

Peter Piper

Peter Piper picked a peck of pickled pepper;
Did Peter Piper pick a peck of pickled pepper?
If Peter Piper picked a peck of pickled pepper,
Where's the peck of pickled pepper
Peter Piper picked?

Anon.

Dick's Dog

Dick had a dog
The dog dug
The dog dug deep
How deep did Dick's dog dig?

Dick had a duck
The duck dived
The duck dived deep
How deep did Dick's duck dive?

Dick's duck dived as deep as Dick's dog dug.

Trevor Millum

Shop Chat

My shop stocks:

locks, chips,
chopsticks,
watch straps,
traps, tops,
taps, tricks,
ship's clocks,
lipstick and chimney pots.

What does your shop stock?

Sharkskin socks.

Libby Houston

111

Slick Nick's Dog's Tricks

Slick Nick's dog does tricks.
The tricks Nick's dog does are slick.
He picks up sticks, stands on bricks,
Nick's finger clicks, the dog barks SIX!
He picks a mix of doggy bix
then gives Slick Nick thick sloppy licks.
Mick and Rick's dog's not so quick –
kicks the bricks, drops the sticks,
can't bark to six, is in a fix,
gets Mick and Rick to do its tricks,
gets on their wicks despite its mix
of waggy tail and loving licks –
but Slick Nick's dog does tricks.
The tricks Nick's dog does are slick.

David Harmer

Barry and Beryl
the Bubble Gum Blowers

Barry and Beryl the bubble gum blowers
blew bubble gum bubbles as big as balloons.
All shapes and sizes, zebras and zeppelins,
swordfish and sealions, sharks and baboons,
babies and buckets, bottles and biplanes,
buffaloes, bees, trombones and bassoons
Barry and Beryl the bubble gum blowers
blew bubble gum bubbles as big as balloons.

Barry and Beryl the bubble gum blowers
blew bubble gum bubbles all over the place.
Big ones in bed, on backseats of buses,
blowing their bubbles in baths with bad taste,
they blew and they bubbled from breakfast till bedtime
the biggest gum bubble that history traced.
One last big breath . . . and the bubble exploded
bursting and blasting their heads into space.
Yes, Barry and Beryl the bubble gum blowers
blew bubbles that blasted their heads into space.

Paul Cookson

Toboggan

To begin to toboggan, first buy a toboggan,
But don't buy too big a toboggan.
(A too big a toboggan is not a toboggan
To buy to begin to toboggan.)

Colin West

Breakfast for One

Hot thick crusty buttery toast
Buttery toasty thick hot crust
Crusty buttery hot thick toast
Crusty thick hot toasty butter
Thick hot buttery crusty toast
Toasty buttery hot thick crust
Hot buttery thick crusty toast –

With marmalade is how I like it most!

Judith Nicholls

Puns and Wordplay

Puns are plays on words that sound similar or the same but have different meanings. Most jokes are based on puns. For example . . . what do you call a dinosaur with one eye? A Doyouthinkhesaurus.

Sea Shoals See Shows on the Sea Bed

The salmon with a hat on was conducting with a baton
and it tried to tune the tuna fish by playing on its scales
the scales had all been flattened when the tuna fish was sat
   on
on purpose by a porpoise and a school of killer whales.
So the salmon with a hat on fiddled with his baton
while the angelfish got ready to play the tambourine.
Things began to happen when the salmon with a baton
was tapping out a pattern for the band of the marines.

There was a minnow on piano, a prawn with a horn,
an otter on guitar looking all forlorn.
A whale voice choir and a carp with a harp,
a belly-dancing jellyfish jiving with a shark.

The octaves on the octopus played the middle eight
but they couldn't keep in tune with the skiffle-playing skate.
The plaice on the bass began to rock and roll
with the bloater in a boater and a Dover sole.

A clam on castanets, an eel on glockenspiel,
an oyster in a cloister singing with a seal.
The haddock had a headache from the deafening din
and the sword-dancing swordfish sliced off a fin.

A limpet on a trumpet, a flatfish on a flute,
the kipper fell asleep with King Canute.
Barracuda on a tuba sat upon a rock,
the electric eel gave everyone a shock.

The shrimp and the sturgeon, the stingray and the squid
sang a four-part harmony on the seabed.
The crab and the lobster gave their claws a flick,
kept everyone in time with their click click click . . .
kept everyone in time with their click click click . . .
kept everyone in time with their click click click.

Yes, the salmon with a hat on was tapping out a pattern
and things began to happen for the band of the marines.
It was an ocean of commotion of Atlantic proportion
the greatest show by schools of shoals that ever had been
    seen.

Paul Cookson

Have You Read . . .?

Enjoy your Homework   by R.U. Joking
Out for the Count   by I.C. Stars
Cliff-Top Rescue   by Justin Time
A Year in Space   by Esau Mars

Your Turn to Wash Up   by Y. Mee
Off to the Dentist   by U. First
Broken Windows   by E. Dunnett
Pickpocket Pete   by M.T. Purse

Lions on the Loose   by Luke Out
Helping Gran   by B.A. Dear
Ten Ice-creams   by I. Segovia Flaw
Rock Concert   by Q. Here

Judith Nicholls

Wordspinning

Spin pins into nips.
Snap pans into naps.
Mix spit into tips.
Turn parts into traps.

Switch post into stop.
Whisk dear into dare.
Carve hops into shop.
Rip rate into tear.

Twist tame into mate.
Make mean into name.
Juggle taste into state
In the wordspinning game.

John Foster

My Dad is Amazing!

My dad's **amazing** for he can:

make mountains out of molehills,
teach Granny to suck eggs,
make Mum's blood boil
and then drive her up the wall.

My dad's **amazing** for he also:

walks around with his head in the clouds,
has my sister eating out of his hand,
says he's got eyes in the back of his head
and can read me like a book.

But,
the most **amazing** thing of all is:

when he's caught someone red-handed,
first he jumps down their throat
and then he bites their head off!

Ian Souter

Emergensea

The octopus awoke one morning and wondered what
  rhyme it was.
Looking at his alarm-clocktopus
he saw that it had stopped
and it was time to stop having a rest
and get himself dressed.
On every octofoot
he put
an octosocktopus
but in his hurry, one foot got put
not into an octosock
but into an electric plug socket
and the octopus got a nasty electric shocktopus
and had to call the octodoctopus
who couldn't get in
to give any help or medicine
because the door was loctopus.
The octopus couldn't move, being in a state of
  octoshocktopus
so the octodoctopus bashed the door
to the floor
and the cure was as simple as could be:
a nice refreshing cup of seawater.

John Hegley

Sunday in the Yarm Fard

The mat keowed
The mow cooed
The bog darked
The kigeon pooed

The squicken chalked
The surds bang
The kwuck dacked
The burch rells chang

And then, after all the dacking and changing
The chalking and the banging
The darking and the pooing
The keowing and the kooing
There was a mewtiful beaumont
Of queace and pie-ate.

Trevor Millum

122

Three Relatively Silly Poems

1.

I flew in a rocket to **ma's**
and some **mother** planets too,
then **father** into space until
the **son** was out of view.

2.

I remem-**brother** nights like this
with a full moon high in an **uncle**-ouded sky.
We were young. Life was a **grandad** venture.
A **niece twin**ned blew and the air was fresh and dry.

3.

Wife I been itching and twitching
as if **I dad** bad chickenpox?
Because I've got hundreds of **aunts** in my pants
a **nephew** more in my socks.

Nick Toczek

You Tell Me

Here are the football results:
League Division Fun
Manchester United won, Manchester City lost.
Crystal Palace 2 Buckingham Palace 1
Millwall Leeds nowhere
Wolves 8 A cheese roll and had a cup of tea 2
Aldershot 3, Buffalo Bill shot 2
Evertonil, Liverpool's not very well either
Newcastle's Heaven, Sunderland's a very nice place 2
Ipswhich one? You tell me.

Michael Rosen

At the End of School Assembly

Miss Sparrow's lot flew out,
Mrs Steed's lot galloped out,
Mr Bull's lot got herded out,
Mrs Bumble's lot buzzed off.

Miss Rose's class . . . rose,
Mr Beetle's class . . . beetled off,
Miss Storm's class thundered out,
Mrs Frisby's class whirled across the hall.

Mr Train's lot made tracks,
Miss Ferry's lot sailed off,
Mr Roller's lot got their skates on,
Mrs Street's lot got stuck halfway across.

Mr Idle's class just couldn't be bothered,
Mrs Barrow's class were wheeled out,
Miss Stretcher's class were carried out
And
Mrs Brook's class
Simply
trickled away

Simon Pitt

Good Morning, Mr Croco-Doco-Dile

Good morning, Mr Croco-doco-dile,
And how are you today?
I like to see you croco-smoco-smile
In your croco-woco-way.

From the tip of your beautiful croco-toco-tail
To your croco-hoco-head
You seem to me so croco-stoco-still
As if you're croco-doco-dead.

Perhaps if I touch your croco-cloco-claw
Or your croco-snoco-snout,
Or get up close to your croco-joco-jaw
I shall very soon find out.

But suddenly I croco-soco-see
In your croco-oco-eye
A curious kind of croco-gloco-gleam,
So I just don't think I'll try.

Forgive me, Mr Croco-doco-dile
But it's time I was away.
Let's talk a little croco-woco-while
Another croco-doco-day.

Charles Causley

Never Kiss Your Lover

Never kiss your lover at the garden gate
Love is blind, but the neighbours ain't.

Anon.

Jingle Jangle

Jingle jangle
Silver bangle
You look cute
From every angle.

Anon.

Apples are Red

Apples are red
My nose is blue
Standing at the bus stop
Waiting for you.

Anon.

A Note

If for me there is no hope
Send me back a yard of rope.

Anon.

Shape Poems/ Calligrams/ Concrete Verse

A shape poem is a poem where the visual layout of the words reflects the shape or aspect of a subject.

A calligram is a poem where the formation or font of the letters used represent an aspect of the poem, for example, thin, fat, high and so on.

Concrete poems are very similar to shape poems although concrete poems can be presented as sculptures where words or phrases can be repeated to form a block of text. The shape of a concrete poem adds further layers of meaning to the poem.

AND IT'S A . . .

Miller gets the ball and
   d
    r
    i
    b
    l
   e
   s

       d
       o
       w
       n

       the

       w
       i
       n
       g

bas   f   a   a k e   from Smith
et   o f   t c l

Oh no! He's lost it!
                 r
                 i
                 a
                the
                in
                up
                it
             s
                e
                  o
WAIT! He t
     s it to – oh – kcab ti sessap eh.
   d
   a
  e
 h

A lovely c
          u
           r
           v
           i
           n
          g   kick

AND IT'S A . . .

wONDerful S-A-A-A-A-A-A-A-A-A-V-E!

                              Rita Ray

Translation

Miller gets the ball and dribbles
down the wing, beats off a tackle
from Smith. Oh no! He's lost it!
Wait! He toes it up in the air,
heads it to – oh – he passes it
back. A lovely curving kick.
And it's a wonderful save!

The Shape I'm In

Come and see the SHAPE I'm in

TALL as a tale

THIN as a pin

W I D E as a smile

Bright as a tin

I'm sometimes this

and sometimes that

but I'm never ever DULL!!!!!

or

FLAT

James Carter

Rhythm Machine

Soft and

humming -

LOUD

and *strumming* -

Listen to this NEAT refrain!

Add a

TRUMPET

And a

DRUM kit –

why not change the B
        E
          A
            T again?

UP
THE ***VOLUME***

Eardrum priser,

 POP GROUP
syntheSIZER!

Trevor Harvey

136

Somersault

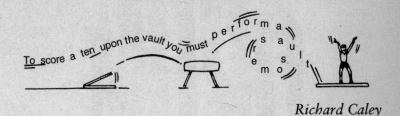

To score a ten upon the vault you must perform a somersault

Richard Caley

Undersea Tea

OLIVER THE OCTOPUS

UNDERNEATH THE SEA

SWIMMING VERY SLOWLY

LOOKING FOR HIS TEA

MAKES A LITTLE BUBBLE

GIVES A LITTLE GRIN

"HI THERE, FISHES!

COME ON IN . . .

Tony Mitton

Cats Can

Cats can s t r e t c h

And cats can curl

Cats can p o u n c e

And twirl twirl

Cats can i t s

And cats can laze

z
z
z

And p u r r r into

A sleepy haze

Coral Rumble

Diamond Poem

Spark
Glows red
In wind's breath.
Struggles for life
Flickers. Dies. Flickers.
Bursts into flame.
Twists and leaps.
Dancing
Fire.

John Foster

In the Bath

When I pull the plug out
with my round and
wrinkly toe,
the water
likes
to
g
u
r
g
l
e

as
it
d
i
s
a
p
p
e
a
r
s

b
e
l
o
w

Andrew Collett

Pyramid

P
EAK
PLACE
PROUDLY
PROVIDING
PRESTIGIOUS
PLUSH PRIVATE
PILED PENTHOUSE
PERFECTLY PLANNED
PANORAMIC POSITION
PART PAYMENT POSSIBLE
PAST PHARAOHS PREFERRED

Dave Calder

Dennis

          D
         E
        N
       N
      I
     S
Dennis is the ice
cream man – He drives
about in his ice cream van
You always know when he's around
Because: a) you can hear
that little tune he plays
from miles away –
and b) everyone
runs outside
screaming
'Hey, it's
Dennis
!!!'

James Carter

Acrostic Poems

If you read the first letter of each line of an acrostic
poem downwards they will often make a word or phrase.
The lines across may consist of one word or a phrase.
Sometimes the key word can be found down the centre
of the poem or even at the end of the line but it is the
arrangement of words and lines around this word that
makes it an acrostic poem.

An Acrostic

A favourite literary devi
Ce is the one whe
Re the first letter
Of each line spell
S out the subject the poe
T wishes to write about.
I must admit, I
Can't see the point myself.

Roger McGough

Giant

Enormous feeder
Loyal minder
Earth remover
Power lifter
Handy blaster
Alarming trumpeter
Nimble rammer
Thunder maker

Early learner
Laughter maker
Easy dozer
Practical joker
Huge destroyer
Ageless wonder
Noisy swimmer
Treetop cropper

Jack Ousbey

Morning Meeting

Fresh dewfall glistens on the lawn;
Roses gleam with tiny pearls:
In the breeze and morning sun
Each petal trembles and uncurls:
Now in the borders all the flowers
Display their charms like dancing girls.

Then I see beside a show
Of bright nasturtiums on the ground

That curious shape: I do not know
How it came or what I've found.
Edging closer then I see

How like the bristles of a brush
Employed for scrubbing floors it looks.
'Do not touch,' it seems to say.
'Great human creature who could crush
Every small insectivore!'
'Have no fear; I'll go away
Only to come back with sweet
Greens and meat for you to eat.'

Vernon Scannell

My Glasses

M – Meaningful
Y – Yes my glasses are meaningful

G – Grip my head at the sides
L – Love is strong so are my glasses
A – Attached to my head at the sides
S – Stop me walking into opticians
S – See through
E – Ever so clean
S – Seven quid

John Hegley

Acrostic

A cross stick?
Can't understand what sir's
Rabbiting
On about.
So I
Thought
I'd
Compose a poem instead.

John Foster

Introducing the . . .

Oggle-eyed
Creepy weirdo
Tough and tetchy
On the lookout
Prowling, pouncing
Up-wrapping
Shell cracker

Patricia Leighton

Estuary

East coast winds
Saltings and sea marsh
Tidal currents ebb and flow
Underfoot, exposed mud banks
Above brent geese honk
Reeds rustle
Yachts skim.

Anita Marie Sackett

Diwali

Diwali lamps are twinkling, twinkling
In the sky and in our homes and hearts.
We welcome all with cheery greetings
And sweets and patterned *rangoli* art.
Lakshmi flies upon her owl tonight;
Incense curls, our future's sparkling bright.

Debjani Chatterjee

Rangoli patterns are drawn at the entrance to a home to welcome visitors.
Lakshmi, the Goddess of Wealth and Good Fortune, blesses the homes
where lamps are lit in her honour.

Crocodile

Crocodile
Resting in the
Ooze, unaware of
Cruel calumnies,
Or rumours, that she eats her offspring
Dozing, waiting for her eggs to hatch
In the blazing sun. Soon it will be time to
Leave this place, lovingly opening
Enormous jaws to carry her babies to the water.

Christine Potter

Seasons

Spring

Springtime casts a spell of green,
Paints flowers opening to the sun.
Rains falls softly, saying 'Wake',
In a fresh world just begun.
New leaves and buds, birds and lambs,
Grow and burst, hatch and run.

Summer

Summer, when we lie on grass
Under shimmer of blue sky.
Murmuring bees, shade of trees,
Matching butterflies flutter by.
Evening holds the scent of flowers,
Racing in lightness, swallows fly.

Autumn

Autumn, when the leaves turn red,
Umber and amber and then fly.
The wispy smoke of bonfires drifts
Upwards in the evening sky.
Morning mists blur scarlet berries,
Nuts and apples drop and die.

Winter

Winter, when your warm breath smokes
In the bitter morning chill.
Night brings frosts that creep and crisp.
Trees are stretching black and still,
Etching patterns where the bright
Robin dares a whistling trill.

Jo Peters

Thin Poems

It may sound obvious but thin poems are poems that are thin, where the text on each line is maybe a few words at the most. Lists lend themselves to thin poems.

Where to Put Your Poem (Daft Draft)

Poems
written
on
pieces
of
string
are
usually
slender
yes
long
and
thin.

Tony Mitton

I Don't Know What to Write

I don't
know what
to write.
My
classmates
seem much
slicker.
If I
write like
this,
I'll fill
my page
much
quicker!

Tracey Blance

MY Team

They're a . . .
Hard-shooting
Firm-booting
Fast-running
Crowd-stunning
Ball-keeping
Nifty-sweeping
Smooth-gliding
Glory-riding
First-rating
Penetrating
Stadium-filling
Opponent-killing
Net-whacking
Post-cracking
Table-topping
Drama-making
RECORD-BREAKING
Sort of team!

Coral Rumble

Crusher

I'm a
huge hy-
draulic
crusher.
Read my
base I'm
made in
Russia.
Oiled out
of a
Texas
gusher.
Piston
puller.
Piston
pusher.
Function
like a
toilet
flusher.
I'm a
huge hy-
draulic
crusher.
Made to
be a
metal
musher.

My sur-
roundings
could be
plusher.
Scrap-yard
mud that
should be
lusher.
I work
slowly.
I'm no
rusher.
I'm a
huge hy-
draulic
crusher.

Nick Toczek

Wrestling with Mum

Mum says, 'Let's fight.'
I say, 'Not tonight.'
But she nabs me, grabs me
twists and Boston Crabs me
lifts me
shifts me
Back Hammer
Body Slammer
Scissor Lock
Forearm Block
Arm Bender
Up Ender
Back Breaker
Widow Maker
Knee Drop
Karate Chop
Leg Split
SUBMIT
NO
Meat Cleaver
Arm Lever
Bear Hug
Finger Tug
Forearm Smash
Death Crash
Head Butt
Upper Cut
Shoulder Barge

Depth Charge
Arm Screw
follow through
Shoulder Press
No
Yes
No
Yes
1
2
3
PINFALL!
'Now tell me. What did you do at school?'

John Coldwell

What Are Little Girls . . .

I'm not
a
sugar and spice
girl
an all-things-nice
girl
a do-as-told
good-as-gold
pretty frock
never shock
girl

I'm
a
slugs and snails
girl
a puppy-dogs'-tails
girl
a climbing trees
dirty knees
hole-in-sock
love-to-shock
girl

cricket bats
and big white rats
crested newts
and football boots

that's what
this little girl's

. . . Made Of.

Adrian Henri

Dandelion Time

Dandelion
Clock tower.
No bell
To tell
The hour.

No tick,
No chime,
No face
To trace
The time.

No glass,
No sands.
Time blown,
Not shown
By hands.

Sue Cowling

Poems About the Senses

These poems reflect aspects of the five senses –
sight, sound, smell, touch and taste.

Five Little Senses All in a Row

You're so sweet! said Lickety Lips,
Keep in touch! said Fingertips
See you soon! said Eye with a wink
Said the nose, *Don't cause a stink!*
Hear me out! said the ears immense,
Together, we make a lot of **SENSE!**

Andrew Fusek Peters

A Poem to Be Spoken Silently . . .

It was so silent that I heard
my thoughts rustle
like leaves in a paper bag . . .

It was so peaceful that I heard
the trees ease off
their coats of bark . . . .

It was so still that I heard
the paving stones groan
as they muscled for space . . .

It was so silent that I heard
a page of this book
whisper to its neighbour,
'Look he's peering at us again . . .'

It was so still that I felt
a raindrop grin
as it tickled the window's pane . . .

It was so calm that I sensed
a smile crack the face
of a stranger . . .

It was so quiet that I heard
the morning earth roll over
in its sleep and doze
for five minutes more . . .

Pie Corbett

Wings

If I had wings
I would touch the fingertips of clouds
and glide on the wind's breath.

If I had wings
    I would taste a chunk of the sun
        as hot as peppered curry.

If I had wings
    I would listen to the clouds of sheep bleat
        that graze on the blue.

If I had wings
    I would breathe deep and sniff
        the scent of raindrops.

If I had wings
    I would gaze at the people
        who cling to the earth's crust.

If I had wings
    I would dream of
        swimming the deserts
            and walking the seas.

Pie Corbett

Sounds

The tiniest sound in the world must be
a little green caterpillar eating his tea.

The spookiest sound in the world must be
a ghost singing songs in a hollow tree.

The noisiest sound in the world must be
thunder pushing mountains into the sea.

The happiest sound in the world must be
our baby chuckling when she plays with me!

Irene Rawnsley

Sounds Like Magic

I listened to a sea-shell
and thought I could hear
the rushing of the waves
inside my ear.

I held an empty egg-shell
close against my head
and thought I heard a pecking chick
hatching from its bed

170

I found a hollow coconut
and listened for a sound
and thought I heard horses' hooves
pounding on the ground.

I took an empty teacup
to see what I might hear
and thought I heard a giant's voice
booming in my ear.

Celia Warren

As Tasty as a Picnic

As salty as the sea,
As crunchy as the sand,
My banana sandwich
is curling in my hand.

As soft as the sun,
As sweet as a grin,
My vanilla ice cream
is dripping down my chin.

Celia Warren

My Hands

Think of all my hands can do,
pick up a pin and do up a shoe,
they can help, they can hurt too,
or paint a summer sky bright blue.

They can throw and they can catch.
They clap the team that wins the match.
If I'm rough my hands can scratch.
If I'm rude my hands can snatch.

Gently, gently they can stroke,
carefully carry a glass of Coke,
tickle my best friend for a joke,
but I won't let them nip and poke.

My hands give and my hands take.
With Gran they bake a yummy cake.
They can mend but they can break.
Think of music hands can make.

Jo Peters

Smelly People

Uncle Oswald smells of tobacco.
Aunt Agatha smells of rope.
Cousin Darren smells of aeroplane glue.
Cousin Tracey smells of soap.

My mum smells of garlic and cabbage.
My dad smells of cups of tea.
My baby sister smells of sick
and my brother of TCP.

Our classroom smells of stinky socks.
Our teacher smells of Old Spice.
I wonder what I smell of?
I'll just have a sniff . . .
hmmm . . . quite nice.

Roger Stevens

New Sights

I like to see a thing I know
Has not been seen before,
That's why I cut my apple through
To look into the core.

It's nice to think, though many an eye
Has seen the ruddy skin,
Mine is the very first to spy
The five brown pips within.

Anon.

I Saw

I saw a peacock with a fiery tail
I saw a blazing comet drop down hail
I saw a cloud with ivy circled round
I saw a sturdy oak creep on the ground
I saw an ant swallow up a whale
I saw a raging sea brim full of ale
I saw a Venice glass sixteen foot deep
I saw a well full of men's tears that weep
I saw their eyes all in a flame of fire
I saw a house as big as the moon and higher
I saw the sun even in the midst of night
I saw the man that saw this wondrous sight.

Anon.

March Dusk

About the hour light wobbles
Between the day and night,

On paving-stones and cobbles
Rain hisses with weak spite

And plane trees dangling bobbles,
Drip leafless from numb height

Where wounded springtime hobbles
That soon will leap with light.

Kit Wright

Modern Poems

This is poetry that isn't constrained by patterns of rhyme or rhythm. It often appears more like prose.

Best Friends

Would a best friend
   Eat your last sweet
   Talk about you behind your back
   Have a party and not ask you?

Mine did.

Would a best friend
   Borrow your bike without telling you
   Deliberately forget your birthday
   Avoid you whenever possible?

Mine did.

Would a best friend
   Turn up on your bike
   Give you a whole packet of your favourite sweets
   Look you in the eye?

Mine did.

Would a best friend say
   Sorry I talked about you behind your back
   Sorry I had a party and didn't invite you
   Sorry I deliberately forgot your birthday
   – I thought you'd fallen out with me

Mine did.

And would a best friend say, simply,
   Never mind
   That's OK.

I did.

                 Bernard Young

My Eyes are Watering

I've got a cold
And that is why
My eyes are watering.

It's nothing to do
With getting caught
When I had planned
To SMASH
The rounders ball
SO FAR
That it would go
Into PERMANENT ORBIT
Round the school.
It would've done, too –
If Lucy Smith
Hadn't RUSHED
To catch it.

'Look at Trevor –
He's having a cry!'
Not true.
I've got a cold
And THAT is why
My eyes are watering.

OK?

Trevor Harvey

Unfolding Bud

One is amazed
By a water-lily bud
Unfolding
With each passing day,
Taking on a richer colour
And new dimensions.

One is not amazed,
At a first glance,
By a poem,
Which is as tight-closed
As a tiny bud.

Yet one is surprised
To see the poem
Gradually unfolding,
Revealing its rich inner self,
As one reads it
Again
And over again.

Naoshi Koriyama

True Confession

On my birthday I wrapped
a big slice of chocolate cake
in pink paper to give
to Miss Twiglington,

but when I got to school
she was horrible to me;
'You haven't worked hard enough,
your spellings are bad

margin crooked,
fingerprints all over'
then she ripped out the page
and made me start again. I thought

'She's not getting that cake.'
When break time came
I ate it myself in the playground
and I didn't care.

Irene Rawnsley

It's Spring

It's spring
And the garden is changing its clothes,
Putting away
Its dark winter suits,
Its dull scarves
And drab brown overcoats.

Now, it wraps itself in green shoots,
Slips on blouses
Sleeved with pink and white blossom,
Pulls on skirts of daffodil and primrose,
Snowdrop socks and purple crocus shoes,
Then dances in the sunlight.

John Foster

I'm Free

This is what is sometimes called free verse.
Free verse need not rhyme, although from time to time it
    may.
It's not the same as weary prose
Which flutters through your letter-box each day
In advert after advert or in the daily news.
You may catch a steady pulse in every line,
Or you may not.
Some lines may, like the last, be short and to the point,
Others, like this, may wander on and on as the poet thinks
    most fit.
Free verse is not, as some might think,
A lazy way to write. To do it well takes care.
Words and thoughts must match,
Must be well carved.
But it seems to me sometimes
That, without the tidy shape of rhythms, lines and rhymes,
Free verse, though it may have wise things to say,
Is harder than other verse
To hold forever in the head.

Perhaps that's why some older folk
Prefer rhymed verse instead?

John Kitching

My Brother

My brother is loud.
His shouts bounce off the walls
like gunshots.
If he was in a strip cartoon
his words would be
in big block capitals
all the time.
He makes everybody else sound quiet.
He's the only person I know
who can speak in a
deafening whisper.

Gus Grenfell

About Knees

Mum doesn't understand about knees,
how they need a smear of mud
to look cool in the playground.
She scrubs them with a flannel.

Mum doesn't understand about knees,
how they always stick out,
and they graze when you fall over.
She fixes plasters across them.

Mum doesn't understand about knees,
how they get the best bruises –
all purple and yellow blotches.
She rubs greasy ointment into them.

Mum doesn't understand about knees,
how they're just right for drawing
beetles on with a green felt tip.
She takes the nail brush to them.

Perhaps Mum should wear shorts next summer,
see what happens to HER knees.
And I'll be ready with the flannel,
the plasters, ointment and nail brush.

                                        Alison Chisholm

New School

In the playground corner
I stand and see:
Girls with skipping ropes,
Boys with footballs
And everyone shouts at once.

In the playground corner
I stand and see:
A teacher looking at his watch,
Cup of coffee in one hand
And a whistle in the other.

In the playground corner
I stand and see:
Big kids sharing jokes and sweets,
One skits our headmaster
And everyone knows everyone else.

In the playground corner
I stand on my own
And wish and wish
I could just go home.

Kevin McCann

Conkers

The boy leapt towards
The branches of the chestnut tree,
Grasped the tempting treasure,
Split the spiky shell
And marvelled at the glowing nut.
'This one's a winner,' he chortled,
Hoarding it into his pocket.

Anita Marie Sackett

Give Yourself a Hug

Give yourself a hug
when you feel unloved

Give yourself a hug
when people put on airs
to make you feel a bug

Give yourself a hug
when everyone seems to give you
a cold-shoulder shrug

Give yourself a hug –
a big big hug

And keep on singing,
'Only one in a million like me
Only one in a million-billion-trillion-zillion
like me.'

Grace Nichols

Billy Doesn't Like School Really

Billy doesn't like school really.
It's not because he can't do the work
but because some of the other kids
don't seem to like him that much.

They call him names
and make up jokes about his mum.

Everyone laughs . . . except Billy.
Everyone laughs . . . except Billy.

They all think it's OK
because it's only a laugh and a joke
and they don't really mean it anyway
but Billy doesn't know that.

Billy doesn't know that
and because of that
Billy doesn't like school really.

Paul Cookson

Den to Let

To let
One self-contained
Detached den.
Accommodation is compact
Measuring one yard square.
Ideal for two eight-year-olds
Plus one small dog
Or two cats
Or six gerbils.
Accommodation consists of:
One living-room
Which doubles as kitchen
Bedroom
Entrance-hall
Dining-room
Dungeon
Space capsule
Pirate boat
Covered wagon
Racing car
Palace
Aeroplane
Junk-room
And look-out post.
Property is southward facing
And can be found
Within a short walking distance
Of the back door

At bottom of garden.
Easily found in the dark
By following the smell
Of old cabbages and tea-bags.
Convenient escape routes
Past rubbish dump
To Seager's Lane
Through hole in hedge,
Or into next door's garden;
But beware of next door's rhinoceros
Who sometimes thinks he's a poodle.
Construction is of
Sound corrugated iron
And roof doubles as shower
During rainy weather.
Being partially underground,
Den makes
A particularly effective hiding place
When in a state of war
With older sisters
Brothers
Angry neighbours
Or when you simply want to be alone.
Some repair work needed
To north wall
Where Mr Spence's foot came through
When planting turnips last Thursday.
With den go all contents
Including:
One carpet – very smelly

One teapot – cracked
One woolly penguin –
No beak and only one wing
One unopened tin
Of sultana pud
One hundred and three Beanos
Dated 1983–1985
And four Rupert annuals.
Rent is free
The only payment being
That the new occupant
Should care for the den
In the manner to which it has become accustomed
And on long summer evenings
Heroic songs of days gone by
Should be loudly sung
So that old and glorious days
Will never be forgotten.

Gareth Owen

Shallow Poem

I've thought of a poem.
I carry it carefully,
nervously, in my head,
like a saucer of milk;
in case I should spill some lines
before I can put it down.

Gerda Mayer

Burying the Dog in the Garden

When we buried
the dog in
the garden on
the grave we put
a cross and
the tall man
next door was
cross.
'Animals have no
souls,' he said.
'They must have animal
souls,' we said. 'No,'
he said and
shook his head.
'Do you need a

193

soul to go
to Heaven?' we
asked. He nodded
his head. 'Yes,'
he said.
'That means my
hamster's not
in Heaven,' said
Kevin. 'Nor is
my dog,' I said.
'My cat could sneak
in anywhere,' said
Clare. And we thought
what a strange place Heaven
must be with
nothing to stroke
for eternity.
We were all
seven.
We decided we
did not want to
go to Heaven.
For that the
tall man next
door is to blame.

Brian Patten

Evening Rain

The evening rain,
Strand by strand is woven into the thought
of the poet.

Ping Hsin
Translated by J. C. Lin

Amulet

Inside the wolf's fang, the mountain of heather.
Inside the mountain of heather, the wolf's fur.
Inside the wolf's fur, the ragged forest.
Inside the ragged forest, the wolf's foot.
Inside the wolf's foot, the stony horizon.
Inside the stony horizon, the wolf's tongue.
Inside the wolf's tongue, the doe's tears.
Inside the doe's tears, the frozen swamp.
Inside the frozen swamp, the wolf's blood.
Inside the wolf's blood, the snow wind.
Inside the snow wind, the wolf's eye.
Inside the wolf's eye, the North star.
Inside the North star, the wolf's fang.

Ted Hughes

Remembrance Days

Ramadan in Pakistan
Is a special time
On Christmas Day in
Jamaica
The sun will always shine,
Diwali in India
Brings all the colours out
And don't forget
In Tibet
Each day
A Poet
Shouts.

Benjamin Zephaniah

At the End of a School Day

It is the end of a school day
  and down the long drive
come bag-swinging, shouting children.
  Deafened, the sky winces.
    The sun gapes in surprise.

Suddenly the runners skid to a stop,
   stand still and stare
at a small hedgehog
   curled-up on the tarmac
     like an old, frayed cricket ball.

A girl dumps her bag, tiptoes forward
   and gingerly, so gingerly
carries the creature
   to the safety of a shady hedge.
     Then steps back, watching.

Girl, children, sky and sun
   hold their breath.
There is a silence,
   a moment to remember
     on this warm afternoon in June.

Wes Magee

Jack Frost is Playing Cards at the Roadside

Jack Frost
Is playing cards with the leaves.
He has spread them out in front of him
And is turning them over one by one,
Telling the Earth's fortune.
Which creatures
Will not wake from hibernation.
Which bulbs
Will burst with cold.
Which plants
Will melt away.
Jack Frost
Sits beside the roadside,
Lonely as ever.
On a twig behind him
A sparrow is sitting mute with cold,
And everything is still and quiet,
Still and quiet.

Across the valley is a village
And the roofs of its little houses
Steam in the morning light,
Which is cold and brief.
And over its inhabitants
Soon clouds will come,
And a net of shadows descend,
And Jack Frost
Will put away his cards,
And the whiteness will pass
And vanish from the grass.

Brian Patten

Mooses

The goofy Moose, the walking house-frame,
Is lost
In the forest. He bumps, he blunders, he stands.

With massy bony thoughts sticking out near his ears –
Reaching out palm upwards, to catch whatever might be
   falling from heaven –
He tries to think,
Leaning their huge weight
On the lectern of his front legs.

He can't find the world!
Where did it go? What does a world look like?
The Moose
Crashes on, and crashes into a lake, and stares at the
  mountain and cries:
'Where do I belong? This is no place!'

He turns dragging half the lake out after him
And charges the cackling underbrush –

He meets another Moose
He stares, he thinks: 'It's only a mirror!'
'Where is the world?' he groans. 'O my lost world!
And why am I so ugly?
And why am I so far away from my feet?'

He weeps.
Hopeless drops drip from his droopy lips.

The other Moose just stands there doing the same.

Two dopes of the deep woods.

Ted Hughes

Empty Head

An idea came
Into my head
So slender
So slight
An idea came
Fleetingly
Fearfully
Came to alight
It wheeled about
Stretched itself out
An idea came
That I wanted to stay
But it brushed my hand
And taking its flight
Through my fingers
Slipped away.

Malick Fall

Haikus

A Japanese form of poetry. Three lines in total, with a
five seven five syllable structure. Seventeen syllables in all.
Often writing with an illustration. Usually about the
seasons. The poem tries to capture a 'word-picture',
a verbal snapshot that echoes a moment of beauty.

Haikus

These poems were written by the well-known Japanese poet Basho (1644–94). In the original Japanese, they are true Haikus, consisting of seventeen syllables. However, in translation, the lines of the poems have been altered so that they no longer follow the Haiku pattern.

Winter downpour –
even the monkey
needs a raincoat.

Old pond,
leap-splash –
a frog.

Friends part
for ever – wild geese
lost in cloud.

Insect song – over
winter's garden
moon's hair-thin.

Wake, butterfly –
it's late, we've miles
to go together.

Violets –
how precious on
a mountain path.

Basho

Haiku

Snowman in a field
listening to the raindrops
wishing him farewell.

Roger McGough

Four Seasons Haiku

1.
yellow rapefields glow;
hedges dipped in mayblossom:
cream in a green bowl.

2.
flags hang limp from masts;
buddleias flop exhausted
on August pavements.

3.
folding up fruit-nets;
already a trawl of leaves
in their green meshes.

4.
take away one word:
a tall chimney collapses
in the winter wood.

Adrian Henri

Haikus

Swaying in the breeze,
Their heads nodding, bluebells ring,
Heralding summer.

Grey as steel, the sea
Shimmers in the fading light:
Day slides into night.

John Foster

Bumble-bee

Why do you bumble?
Are you unsure what to do
In your stripy suit?

Angela Topping

Uphill

My battered bike groans
Two wandering wheels wobble
Twisted spokes shout 'No!'

David Harmer

Proverbial Logic

Where there are pandas
there's bamboo, but the converse
is sadly not true.

Debjani Chatterjee

Haikus

The pen in my hand
Struggles to paint a picture
For your eyes to see.

Oystered haiku words.
All seventeen syllables:
Grit to grow bright pearls.

The shell on my desk
Is tiny, faded with dust,
But still sings wide seas.

John Kitching

NoHaiku

I'm sorry to say
that I really don't feel like
a haiku today.

Adrian Henri

Policeman Haiku

'ello 'ello 'e
llo 'ello 'ello 'ello
What 'ave we 'ere then?

Roger Stevens

Lowku Haiku

If a poem has
Just sixteen syllables
Is it a lowku?

Roger Stevens

Haiku

To convey one's mood
in seventeen syllables
is very diffic

John Cooper Clarke

Tankas

A tanka is another Japanese poem based on the haiku but with two extra lines. So, the syllable pattern is now 5, 7, 5, 7, 7. The poems try to capture the essence of a moment, usually mentioning one of the seasons in some way.

Silver Aeroplane

Silver aeroplane
Speeds across the summer sky
Leaving in its wake
Trails of vapour: white scribblings
On a page of blue paper.

John Foster

Tanka 1

A pool of sunlight
Bathes the stormy evening bay.
A lonely heron
Stands still, a cunning statue,
Waiting for unwary fish.

Tanka 2

Bushes white with frost;
Cobwebs straining winter mist;
Ponds skinned with thin ice
Hide the ghosts of golden fish.
When will gentle spring return?

John Kitching

Red

When we buried Red
the sunlight stroked his smooth coat
and gentled his bed,
because even in death
the soft, petting day loved him.

Coral Rumble

When Leaves Pile Up

When leaves pile up
and scatter through the garden,
I start to worry.
It is time for a bonfire
to set ideas alight.

Jill Townsend

Two Tankas

Tanka is a form
Of poetry from Japan,
Where the syllables
Are counted in a strict way –
Five, seven, five, seven, sev . . .

My school is a clock
Measuring out the subjects
I must learn each day –
Reading, writing and arith . . .
Sorry! Time's up. I must go.

Jack Ousbey

An Old Cat is Annoyed By a Dove

'You pompous, grey bird,
Why do you waddle and peck
Just out of my reach?'

'You are too old to catch me',
it cooed sweetly, cruelly.

David Orme

Cinquains

Like a haiku a cinquain has a standard syllable pattern.
It was invented by Adelaide Crapsey, has a total of
22 syllables, 5 lines and a sequence of 2, 4, 6, 8, 2. The
last line is often used to add impact or a twist to the poem.

Cinquains

This was
Invented by
Adelaide Crapsey, an
American poet, and has
Six lines.

Just like
Learning the two
Times table – 2 – 4 – 6
8 – the syllables for each line
then two.

Paul Cookson

Birds of a Feather

My cat
is old. All she
wants is food, warmth and a
comfy knee. My old cat's a home bird.
Like me.

Bernard Young

On-side Cinquain

The ball
went splat against
the garage wall then bounced
down to my right toe. Goalie had
no chance!

Matt Simpson

School Trip

Line up
search in panic
for partner on the coach.
An odd number – one left over
Why me?

Tracey Blance

Five Lines for Halloween

Windows
At Halloween
Glowing with pumpkin light
Grant us protection from evil
Tonight.

Sue Cowling

Cinquains

Fat troll
Under the bridge
Lurking in the darkness
Hears the trip-trap, trip-trap, trip-trap,
Dinner!

Billy goat
Over the bridge
Strutting in the sunshine
Makes the trip-trap, trip-trap, trip-trap,
No fear!

Troll-goat
Both on the bridge
Staring at each other.
Each says, 'I want to eat you up!'
Splash! Splash!

Gervase Phinn

Cinquains

Redwings
migrating south
descend on the garden
strip the cotoneaster bush
then go.

Leaves swirl
on street corners.
Black polythene is wrapped
round the lamppost like a huge bat
flapping.

Come on
you blues! shouts my
replica kit blowing
on the line. Shirt, shorts, but only
one sock.

Gus Grenfell

Cinquain

And so
As evening falls
I close the curtains on
The empty bed. And shadows creep
Inside.

Valerie Bloom

Cinquain Prayer, February Night

On this
cold night I kneel
with thanks for catkins, pale
green under the lamplight by the
roadside.

Fred Sedgwick

Yo Yo

Yo yo.
Make it fall down
then come back up again.
Down is easy but coming back?
Failure.

Angela Topping

Kennings

These started off in Old English and Norse poetry
where something is described without using its name,
for example, stick fetcher = dog. Anglo Saxons often used
kennings to name their swords: Throat slitter. So, a poem
made from kennings would be a list of expressions about
one subject. More often than not each item on this list is
made up of two words.

Guess Who?

Horse rider
Joust glider
Music maker
Floor shaker
Tennis prancer
Heavy dancer
Diet hater
Serial dater
Dandy dresser
Wife stresser
Church leader
Poor breeder
Nifty speaker
Divorce seeker
Armour filler
Wife killer
Monk basher
Law smasher
Banquet boozer
Bad loser.

Coral Rumble

Answer: Henry VIII

227

Squirrel

Woodland racer
Acorn chaser

Tree shaker
Acorn taker

Nut cracker
Acorn snacker

Sky rider
Acorn hider

Winter snoozer
Acorn loser

Spring reminder
Acorn finder:

One grey squirrel.

Celia Warren

Eight Swords

Death Bringer
Fear Striker
Starlight Catcher
Body Halver
Blood Letter
Mercy Killer
Head Splitter
Flesh Carver

Roger Stevens

Penguin

Seal-teaser
Fish-seizer
Ice-lander
Storm-stander
Egg-cuddler
Warmhuddler
Long-waiter –
Bellyskater!

Sue Cowling

April

Bud bursting
Brightly showering
Nest building
Daffodil flowering
New life of a month.

John Cotton

Teacher

Loud shouter
Deep thinker
Rain hater
Coffee drinker

Spell checker
Sum ticker
Line giver
Nit picker

Ready listener
Trouble carer
Hometime lover
Knowledge sharer

Paul Cookson

Riddles

A poem or verse which forms a puzzle.
They often have several clues to build up the picture
of the puzzle to be solved.

What Am I?

I have no colour,
not even white,
but sometimes I'm wide and blue.
Sometimes I'm still,
and sometimes I rush,
and I can fall down on you.

I can change my shape,
I often do,
but I'm hard to hold in your hand.
You need me to make
your castle stand up
when you're playing in the sand.

I haven't much taste
but on a hot day
your tongue's hanging out for me.
Then I am cold,
but I can be hot
when I'm in your mum's cup of tea.

What am I?

Jo Peters

Answer: Water

Teaser

What kind of ants
tear down trees?
What kind of ants
roll in mud
to take their ease?
What kind of ants
have four knees?
What kind of ants
flap their ears
in the breeze?
What kind of ants
spell their name
with two 'e's?
Sh! Don't tell.
It's a tease.

Tony Mitton

Answer: Elephant

Animal Riddle

Like a small **B**ear
                    bundles over the dark road,
            brushes p**A**st the front gate,
                    as if she owns the joint.
        rolls the **D**ustbin,
                    like an expert barrel-rider
tucks into yesterday's **G**arbage,
                    crunches worms for titbits.
            wak**E**s us from deep sleep,
                    blinks back at torchlight.
    our midnight feaste**R**,

                    ghost-friend,
                    moon-lit,
                    zebra bear.

                                    Pie Corbett

Riddle

My first is in fish but not in chip.
My second in teeth but not in lip.
My third's in potato but not in plum.
My fourth's in mouth and also in thumb.
My fifth is in pear but not in cherry.
My sixth is in bacon but not in berry.
My last is in chocolate but not in crumble.
Sometimes when I'm empty you'll hear me rumble.

John Foster

Answer: Stomach

Riddle

I am at your beginning and your end.
I dog your footsteps
And cannot be shaken off.
Though I fade from view
You are never alone.
So silent that you often forget me.
I am still there,
Your constant dark spy and companion.

John Cotton

Answer: Shadow

Riddle – What Am I?

My first is in cover but not in lid
My second in octopus, not in squid
My third is in marmalade, also in jam
And my fourth is in pork yet never in ham
My fifth is in uncle and also in aunt
My sixth's first in treacle and fifth when in plant
My seventh is in every, eve and ewe twice
Whilst my last is in curry as well as in rice.

What am I?

Richard Caley

Answer: Computer

Riddle

In the log-cabin,
A hundred guardsmen are lying asleep.
Ssh! The door slides open.
Enter a pink-headed monster.
Quickly she grabs a guardsman,
Dashes his head on the wall.
She tries him with fancy hair-styles,
First an orange wig,
Then a black crew-cut.

Leo Aylen

Answer: Striking a match

Riddle # 1

Your father's father's dark and tall.
His movements all are rather small.
His hands on his face, his back to the wall,
he knows his place, it's in the hall.

So ends my game . . . so what's his name?
It's time to tell, which he tells well.

Nick Toczek

Answer: Grandfather clock

Riddle # 2

Who were the soldiers
tall and erect
who came to your door
while you still slept?

Who were the soldiers
pale and thin
who never knocked
to be let in
but stood on guard
with hats of tin?

Nick Toczek

Answer: Milk bottles

Limericks

These poems are comic verses with five lines.
Usually they have a syllable pattern of 8, 8, 6, 6, 8 and
the rhyme scheme A, A, B, B, A. They often begin with
a line like *There was a young fellow from . . .*

Limerick

A limerick's cleverly versed –
The second line rhymes with the first;
The third one is short,
The fourth's the same sort,
And the last line is often the worst.

John Irwin

Limerick

A bald-headed man from Dundee
Lost his wig, in a wind, in a tree;
When he looked up and spied it,
A hen was inside it,
And it laid him an egg for his tea.

Jack Ousbey

Spring Magic!

What a fearless magician is Spring –
you really can't teach her a thing!
In she sneaks on a breeze,
draws the leaves from their trees . . .
just when Winter thought *he* was still King!

Judith Nicholls

Limerick

An intrepid young woman from Stock
climbed a precipitous rock.
She fell from the peak
and when able to speak,
said, 'That didn't half give me a shock.'

Marian Swinger

Short Visit, Long Stay

The school trip was a special occasion
But we never reached our destination
Instead of the Zoo
I was locked in the loo
On an M62 Service Station.

Paul Cookson

Explosive Tale

There was a volcano called Dot –
once on maps just a miniscule spot.
But, 'I'm hungry!' Dot grumbled
as her insides rumbled.
'And what's more, I'm feeling quite hot!'

Judith Nicholls

There Was a Young Lad of St Just

There was a young lad of St Just
Who ate apple pie till he bust;
It wasn't the fru-it
That caused him to do it,
What finished him off was the crust.

Anon.

There Was an Old Man

There was an Old Man with a beard,
Who said, 'It is just as I feared! –
    Two Owls and a Hen,
    four Larks and a Wren,
Have all built their nests in my beard!'

Edward Lear

Family Problems

I have a strange Auntie called Jean.
She's quite tall and thin as a bean.
On bright sunny days,
When she's standing sideways,
Aunt Jean cannot even be seen.

John Kitching

Clerihews

A four-line comic verse of two rhyming couplets.
The lines can be of any length but the first involves the
name of the person being written about. Invented by
E. Clerihew Bentley who died in 1956.

Edmund

Edmund Clerihew Bentley
Invented the type of poem you are reading presently.
Two comic rhyming couplets about a person where the
  length isn't fixed
Then he died in nineteen fifty-six.

Paul Cookson

Little Miss Muffet

Little Miss Muffet
Sat on a tuffet.
The poor little spider
Lay chewed up inside her.

Andrea Shavick

Michael Owen

Michael Owen, Michael Owen
Runs so fast his boots are glowing.
Kicks the ball for all his worth
Now it's orbiting the Earth.

Roger Stevens

Clerihew

Napoleon Bonaparte
Was France's own Braveheart.
But he didn't quite know what to do
At Waterloo.

John Kitching

Neil Armstrong

Neil Armstrong
Wasn't on the Moon for long.
But in that time he left behind
A giant footprint for mankind.

John Foster

Count Dracula

Count Dracula
At blood-sports is quite spectacular.
He hunts for prey at dead of night
And always gets in the first bite.

John Foster

Clerihew

Jane Austen
Got lost in
Stoke-on-Trent
Moral: She shouldn't have went.

Roger McGough

Lists

List poems use a repeating line or phrase, or act like a list.

Ten Things Found in a Wizard's Pocket

A dark night.
Some words that nobody could ever spell.
A glass of water full to the top.
A large elephant.
A vest made from spiders' webs.
A handkerchief the size of a car park.
A bill from the wand shop.
A bucket full of stars and planets, to mix with the dark night.
A bag of magic mints you can suck for ever.
A snoring rabbit.

Ian McMillan

Locker Inspection

JONES D.
Let's take a look –
What have we here?
A metal hook!
A wooden leg,
A cannonball.
A keg of rum
And that's not all –
A lump of lead
On a length of string,
Dead men's fingers,
A diamond ring,
A dagger, a skull,
An old sea chest –
Of the lockers I've seen, Davy,
Yours is best!

Sue Cowling

Things I'd Do If It Weren't For Mum

Live on cola, crisps and cake.
Trade the gerbil for a snake.
Fall asleep in front of the telly.
Only wash when I'm really smelly.
Leave my clothes all scattered about.
Play loud music, scream and shout.
Do what I feel like with my hair.
Throw tantrums. Belch loud. Swear.
Paint my bedroom red and black.
Leave the dishes in a stack.
Find out what it's like to be me.
Let this list grow long . . . Get free!

PS Take my savings in my hand.
Buy a ticket to Laserland.

Tony Mitton

Things I'd Do If It Weren't For My Son

Drink my morning tea in peace and quiet.
Practice yoga. Go on a diet.
Paint his room in almond white.
Dismantle the strobe light.
Give the gerbil cage away.
Keep the telly off all day.
Get the kitchen nice and clean.
Take a break from the washing machine.
Stack the CDs back on the shelf.
Have the house completely to myself.
When it's tea-time, not bother to cook.
Phone for a pizza and read my book.

PS Go for a walking holiday in the hills.
No theme parks, laser quests or other thrills.

Tony Mitton

Younger Brother

He collects bottle tops,
Toilet roll holders,
Dead insects,
Bits of rock and stones
Of interesting shapes and colours,
Half-made models,
Stickers, badges, pencils,
Feathers, germinating seeds,
Used socks (under the bed),
Broken saucers that he never mends,
Torch batteries, glass marbles,
Oh – and friends.

Trevor Millum

The Model We're Making in Class with Miss

Scissors, glue, yoghurt pots,
sellotape, a cornflake box,
egg cartons, bottle tops,
rubber gloves, dad's old socks.

Cardboard and hardboard
and my brother's dartboard.
Polythene and plasticine
and my mother's magazine.

Walking sticks, building bricks
lipsticks and Prittsticks,
silly string, safety pins,
lots and lots of other things.

Plastic, elastic,
we're enthusiastic,
mould it and fold it
then we'll plaster cast it.
mould it and fold it
and it will be fantastic.

Add a bit of that, then a bit of this
for the model we're making in class with Miss.
Stick it on that, stick it on this
for the model we're making
the model we're making
the model we're making in class with Miss
the model we're making
the model we're making
the model we're making in class with . . . Miss.

Paul Cookson

The Teacher's Day in Bed

Our teacher's having a day in bed –
She's sent her pets to school instead!

There's . . .

A parrot to read the register,
A crocodile to sharpen the pencils,
A canary to teach singing,
An adder to teach maths,
An octopus to make the ink,
An elephant to hoover the floor,
An electric eel to make the computer work,
A giraffe to look for trouble at the back,
A tiger to keep order at the front,
A reed bunting (can't you guess?
to help with reeding, of course!),
A secretary bird to run the office
A piranha fish to give swimming lessons
(Glad I'm off swimming today!),
A zebra to help with crossing the road,
Oh, and a dragon to cook the sausages.

I bet that none of you ever knew
Just how many things a teacher can do!

David Orme

Socks

My local Gents' Outfitter stocks
The latest line in snazzy socks:
Black socks, white socks,
Morning, noon and night socks,
Grey socks, green socks,
Small, large and in between socks,
Blue socks, brown socks,
Always-falling-down socks,
Orange socks, red socks,
Baby socks and bed socks;
Purple socks, pink socks,
What-would-people-think socks,
Holey socks and frayed socks,
British Empire-made socks,
Long socks, short socks,
Any-sort-of-sport socks,
Thick socks, thin socks,
And 'these-have-just-come-in' socks.

Socks with stripes and socks with spots,
Socks with stars and polka dots,
Socks for ankles, socks for knees,
Socks with twelve-month guarantees,
Socks for aunties, socks for uncles,
Socks to cure you of carbuncles,
Socks for nephews, socks for nieces,
Socks that won't show up their creases,
Socks whose colour glows fluorescent,
Socks for child or adolescent,
Socks for ladies, socks for gents,
Socks for only fifty pence.

Socks for winter, socks for autumn,
Socks with garters to support 'em.
Socks for work and socks for leisure,
Socks hand-knitted, made-to-measure,
Socks of wool and polyester,
Socks from Lincoln, Leeds and Leicester,
Socks of cotton and elastic,
Socks of paper, socks of plastic,
Socks of silk-embroidered satin,
Socks with mottoes done in Latin,
Socks for soldiers in the army,
Socks to crochet or macramé,
Socks for destinations distant,
Shrink-proof, stretch-proof, heat-resistant.

Baggy socks, brief socks,
Union Jack motif socks,
Chequered socks, tartan socks,
School or kindergarten socks,
Sensible socks, silly socks,
Frivolous and frilly socks,
Impractical socks, impossible socks,
Drip-dry machine-only-washable socks,
Bulgarian socks, Brazilian socks,
There seem to be over a million socks!

With all these socks, there's just one catch –
It's hard to find a pair that match.

Colin West

Vegan Delight

Ackees, chapatties
Dumplins an nan,
Channa an rotis
Onion uttapam,
Masala dosa
Green callaloo
Bhel an samosa
Corn an aloo.
Yam an cassava
Pepperpot stew,
Rotlo an guava
Rice an tofu,
Puri, paratha
Sesame casserole,
Brown eggless pasta
An brown bread rolls.

Soya milked muesli
Soya bean curd,
Soya sweet sweeties
Soya's de word,
Soya bean margarine
Soya bean sauce,
What can mek medicine?
Soya of course.
Soya meks yoghurt
Soya ice-cream,
Or soya sorbet

Soya reigns supreme,
Soya sticks liquoriced
Soya salads
Try any soya dish
Soya is bad.

Plantain an tabouli
Cornmeal pudding
Onion bhajee
Wid plenty cumin,
Breadfruit an coconuts
Molasses tea
Dairy free omelettes
Very chilli.
Ginger bread, nut roast
Sorrell, paw paw,
Cocoa an rye toast
I tek dem on tour,
Drinking cool maubi
Meks me feel sweet,
What was dat question now?

What do we eat?

Benjamin Zephaniah

Things I Have Been Doing Lately

Things I have been doing lately:
Pretending to go mad
Eating my own cheeks from the inside
Growing taller
Keeping a secret
Keeping a worm in a jar
Keeping a good dream going
Picking a scab on my elbow
Rolling the cat up in a rug
Blowing bubbles in my spit
Making myself dizzy
Holding my breath
Pressing my eyeballs so that I become temporarily blind
Being very nearly ten
Practising my signature . . .

Saving the best till last.

Allan Ahlberg

Some Favourite Words

Mugwump, chubby, dunk and whoa,
Swizzle, doom and snoop,
Flummox, lilt and afterglow,
Gruff, bamboozle, whoop
And nincompoop.

Wallow, jungle, lumber, sigh,
Ooze and zodiac,
Innuendo, lullaby,
Ramp and mope and quack
And paddywhack.

Moony, undone, lush and bole,
Inkling, tusk, guffaw,
Waspish, croon and cubby-hole,
Fern, fawn, dumbledore
And many more . . .

Richard Edwards

Hedgehog Hiding at Harvest in Hills Above Monmouth

Where you hide
    moon-striped grass ripples like tiger skin
where you hide
    the dry ditch rustles with crickets

where you hide
    the electricity pylon saws and sighs
    and the combine harvester's headlight
    pierces the hedges

where you hide
    in your ball of silence
    your snorts muffled
    your squeaks and scuffles
    gone dumb

    a foggy moon sails over your head,
    the stars are nipped in the bud

where you hide
    you hear the white-faced owl hunting
    you count the teeth of the fox.

Helen Dunmore

Inside the Morning

Inside the morning is a bird,
Inside the bird is a song,
Inside the song is a longing.

And the longing is to fill the morning.

June Crebbin

Making the Countryside

Take a roll of green,
Spread it under a blue or blue-grey sky,
Hollow out a valley, mould hills.

Let a river run through the valley,
Let fish swim in it, let dippers
Slide along its surface.

Sprinkle cows in the water-meadows,
Cover steep banks with trees,
Let foxes sleep beneath and owls above.

Now, let the seasons turn,
Let everything follow its course.
Let it be.

June Crebbin

Yes

A smile says: Yes.
A heart says: Blood.
When the rain says: Drink,
The earth says: Mud.

The kangaroo says: Trampoline.
Giraffes say: Tree.
A bus says: Us,
While a car says: Me.

Lemon trees say: Lemons.
A jug says: Lemonade.
The villain says: You're wonderful.
The hero: I'm afraid.

The forest says: Hide and Seek.
The grass says: Green and Grow.
The railway says: Maybe.
The prison says: No.

The millionaire says: Take.
The beggar says: Give.
The soldier cries: Mother!
The baby sings: Live.

The river says: Come with me.
The moon says: Bless.
The stars say: Enjoy the light.
The sun says: Yes.

Adrian Mitchell

A Minute to Midnight

A minute to midnight
and all is still.

For example, these are things that are still:
ornaments, coins, lamp-posts,
the cooker, Major Clark's Home for Old Folk
(just opposite our house, which is also still),
the newsagents, a hut, soap, tractors,
freshly ironed trousers draped over the chair.

A minute to midnight
and all is still
except for the things that are moving.

Like, for example,
rivers, clouds, leaves, flags,
creaky windmills, lungs, birds' feathers,
digital clocks, grass, the wind,
non-sleeping animals (especially wolves),

planet Earth, the moon, satellites in space,
toenails (well they grow, don't they),
videos that are set to record
programmes in the middle of the night,
washing lines,
mobiles above babies' cots –
and babies' eyelids, they always flicker.

John Rice

Alphabet Poems

Poems where the letters of the alphabet play an integral part of the structure of the poem. Usually the letters appear in chronological order and may be a list or sometimes a selection of phrases, for example, *A Brilliant Cat Declared Every Frightened Gerbil Homeless . . .*

A to Z

A up said me dad,
B off to bed with you.
C it's half past eight and I've
Decided that from now on it's bed before nine.
E can't be serious I thought.
F he carries on like this I'll never see any TV
G I'll lose my grasp of American slang.
H not fair.
I won't go.
J think I should protest?
K I will.
L o said me dad,
M not standing for this
N y kid thinks he can disobey me has got another think
    coming.
O yes he has!
P, then wash your hands and face, do your teeth and
    straight to bed.
Q then, your sisters will have finished soon.
R you ready yet? Wash that face properly
S pecially round your nose. It's disgusting.
T? No you can't. If you drink tea now you will wet the bed
U will you know.
V end of a perfect day. Now I'll tuck you in
W up to save space. Then I can fit your brother in too –
    and the dog and hamster. There you all fit in.
Xactly
Y don't you like it? It's cosy, space-saving, economical.

Go to sleep. Not a peep. Do exactly as I
ZZZZZZZZZZZZZZZzz.

Michaela Morgan

The You Can Be A B C

You can be
an artistic Actor or a brainy Barrister
a clever Conductor or a dynamic Dancer
an evil Enemy or a fantastic Friend
a green-fingered Gardener or a healing Herbalist
an interesting Inventor or a jovial jolly Juggler
a keen Kitchen-designer or a loggerheaded Lumberjack
a melodious Musician or a neat Newsreader
an over-the-top Opera singer or a princely-paid Pop star
a quipping Quiz-master or a rich Rugby-player
a serious Scientist or a typewriting Traveller
an uppity Umpire or a vigorous Vet
a wonderful Winner or an expert Xylophonist
a yelling Yachtsperson or a zealous Zoologist.

Roger Stevens

A Monster Alphabet

A is for   **ALIEN** arriving by air
B is for   **BASILISK** with the deadliest stare
C is for   **CYCLOPS**, he's only one eye
D is for   **DRAGON**, he'll light up the sky
E is for   **EXTRATERRESTIAL CREATURES**
F is for   **FRANKENSTEIN** of the frightening features
G is for   **GRIFFIN**, a lion with a beak
H is for   **HYDRA**, the many-headed freak
I is for the **INVISIBLE SPIRITS** of night
J is for   **JACK-O-LANTERN**, that bright little sprite
K is for   **KELPIE**, with the great shining teeth
L is for   **LOCH NESS** and the **MONSTER** beneath
M is for   **MERMAID** who appears from the deep
N is for   **NIGHTMARE** that troubles our sleep
O is for   **OPERA PHANTOM** who sings
P is for   **PHOENIX** with fiery wings
Q is for   **QUASIMODO** who swings from his bell
R is for   **ROC**, the great bird of Hell
S is for   **SANDMAN**, he'll steal every dream
T is for   **TROLL** 'neath the bridge by the stream
U is for   **UNICORN** with her long horn of gold
V is for   **VAMPIRE** in his tomb dark and cold
W is for   **WEREWOLF** who howls 'neath the sky
X is for   **XANTHUS** the horse that can fly
Y is for   **YETI**, that abominable beast
Z is for   **ZOMBIE** the last, but not least.

Gervase Phinn

An Alphabet of Horrible Habits

A is for Albert who makes lots of noise

B is for Bertha who bullies the boys

C is for Cuthbert who teases the cat

D is for Dilys whose singing is flat

E is for Enid who's never on time

F is for Freddy who's covered in slime

G is for Gilbert who never says thanks

H is for Hannah who plans to rob banks

I is for Ivy who slams the front door

J is for Jacob whose jokes are a bore

K is for Kenneth who won't wash his face

L is for Lucy who cheats in a race

M is for Maurice who gobbles his food

N is for Nora who runs about nude

O is for Olive who treads on your toes

P is for Percy who *will* pick his nose

Q is for Queenie who won't tell the truth

R is for Rupert who's rather uncouth

S is for Sibyl who bellows and bawls

T is for Thomas who scribbles on walls

U is for Una who fidgets too much

V is for Victor who talks double Dutch

W is for Wilma who won't wipe her feet

X is for Xerxes who never is neat

Y is for Yorick who's vain as can be

and Z is for Zoe who doesn't love me.

Colin West

A Who'Z Who of the Horrible House

Inside
the
Horrible
House
there is
an awful aquamarine apparition abseiling
a bug-eyed beige bogeyman boxing
a cackling crimson cockroach creeping
a disgusting damson Dracula dancing
an eerie emerald elf electrocuting
a floppy flame Frankenstein fencing
a grotty green ghost groaning
a haunting hazel hag hammering
an insane indigo imp ice-screaming
a jittery jade jackal juggling
a kinky khaki king knitting
a loony lime leprechaun lassooing
a monocled maroon madman marching
a nightmarish navy nastie nipping
an outrageous orange ogre oozing
a phoolish purple phantom phoning
a quadruple quicksilver quagga quaking
a revolting red rattlesnake rock 'n' rolling
a spotty scarlet spectre spitting
a terrible turquoise troll trampolining
an ugly umber uncle umpiring
a violent violet vampire vibrating
a whiskery white werewolf windsurfing

an eXcitable xanthic eXoskeleton eXploding
a yucky yellow yak yelling
a zitty zinc zombie zapping
inside
the
Horrible
House!

Wes Magee

Prayers

Verses, poems and structures used when praying.
These can be for the single or collective voice.

Let No One Steal Your Dreams

Let no one steal your dreams
Let no one tear apart
The burning of ambition
That fires the drive inside your heart.

Let no one steal your dreams
Let no one tell you that you can't
Let no one hold you back
Let no one tell you that you won't.

Set your sights and keep them fixed
Set your sights on high
Let no one steal your dreams
Your only limit is the sky.

Let no one steal your dreams
Follow your heart
Follow your soul
For only when you follow them
Will you feel truly whole.

Set your sights and keep them fixed
Set your sights on high
Let no one steal your dreams
Your only limit is the sky.

Paul Cookson

Children's Prayer

Let the teachers of our class
Set us tests that we all pass.
Let them never ever care
About what uniform we wear.
Let them always clearly state
It's OK if your homework's late.
Let them say it doesn't matter
When we want to talk and chatter.

Let our teachers shrug and grin
When we make an awful din.
Let them tell us every day
There are no lessons. Go and play.
Let them tell our mum and dad
We're always good and never bad.
Let them write in their report
We are the best class they have taught!

John Foster

Prayer

Teach me the value
of what I own,
of what I eat,
of this earth
and of its people.

Help me to remember
whose world it is
why you created it
and why you created
me.

Rupert M. Loydell

The Lord's Prayer

Our Father which art in heaven,
Hallowed be thy name.
The kingdom come.
Thy will be done, in earth as it is in heaven.
Give us this day our daily bread.
And forgive us our trespasses.
As we forgive them that trespass against us.
And lead us not into temptation.
But deliver us from evil.
Thine is the kingdom,
and the power, and the glory,
for ever
Amen.

Matthew 6:9–13
King James Bible

Psalm 23
A Psalm of David.

The Lord *is* my shepherd; I shall not want.

He maketh me to lie down in green pastures: he leadeth me beside the still waters.

He restoreth my soul: he leadeth me in the paths of righteousness for his name's sake.

Yea, though I walk through the valley of the shadow of death, I will fear no evil: for thou *art* with me; thy rod and thy staff they comfort me.

Thou preparest a table before me in the presence of mine enemies: thou anointest my head with oil; my cup runneth over.

Surely goodness and mercy shall follow me all the days of my life: and I will dwell in the house of the LORD for ever.

Psalm 23:1–6
King James Bible

Hanukkah

Light the candles
Me and you
One, two

Pray for peace
Evermore
Three, four

Hold hands
Hug and kiss
Five, six

Always love
Never hate
Seven, eight.

Andrea Shavick

A Bedtime Prayer

Protect me from vampires
Protect me from ghouls
Protect me from phantoms
And howling werewolves
Protect me from witches
Protect me from ghosts
Protect me from brother Sid
I fear him the most.

Richard Caley

Iroquois Prayer

We return thanks to our mother, the earth,
　which sustains us.
We return thanks to the rivers and streams,
　which supply us with water.
We return thanks to all herbs, which furnish
　medicines for the cure of our diseases.
We return thanks to the corn, and to her sisters,
　the beans and squashes, which give us life.
We return thanks to the bushes and trees,
　which provide us with fruit.
We return thanks to the wind, which,
　moving the air, has banished diseases.
We return thanks to the moon and stars,
　which have given to us their light
　when the sun was gone.
We return thanks to our grandfather Hé-no,
　that he has protected his grandchildren from
　witches and reptiles, and has given to us his rain.
We return thanks to the sun, that he has looked upon
　the earth with a beneficent eye.
Lastly, we return thanks to the Great Spirit,
　in whom is embodied all goodness, and who
　directs all things for the good of his children.

Anon.

For a Little Love

For a little love, I would go to the end of the world
I would go with my head bare and feet unshod
I would go through ice, but in my soul forever May,
I would go through the storm, but still hear the
   blackbird sing
I would go through the desert, and have pearls of dew
   in my heart.
For a little love, I would go to the end of the world,
Like the one who sings at the door and begs.

Jaroslav Vrchlicky,
translated from the Czech by
Vera Fusek Peters and Andrew Fusek Peters

The Prayer of the Cat

Lord,
I am a cat,
It is not, exactly, that I have something to ask of You!
No –
I ask nothing of anyone –
but,
if You have by some chance, in some celestial barn,
a little white mouse,
or a saucer of milk,
I know someone who would relish them.
Wouldn't you like some day
to put a curse on the whole race of dogs?
If so I should say,

Amen.

Carmen Bernos de Gasztold,
translated from the French by Rumer Godden

Hurt No Living Thing

Hurt no living thing,
Ladybird nor butterfly,
Nor mouth with dusty wing,
Nor cricket chirping cheerily,
Nor grasshopper, so light of leap,
Nor dancing gnat,
Nor beetle fat,
Nor harmless worms that creep.

Christina Rossetti

Pied Beauty

Glory be to God for dappled things –
  For skies of couple-colour as a brinded cow;
    For rose-moles all in stipple upon trout that swim;
Fresh-firecoal chestnut-falls; finches' wings;
  Landscape plotted and pieced – fold, fallow, and plough;
    And all trades, their gear and tackle and trim.

All things counter, original, spare, strange;
  Whatever is fickle, freckled (who knows how?)
    With swift, slow; sweet, sour; adazzle, dim;
He fathers-forth whose beauty is past change:
                    Praise him.

Gerard Manley Hopkins

Epitaphs

These are usually found on tombstones and are about
people or pets that have died. They usually try to sum
up a feeling about the deceased or an aspect of their
character. The more humorous type usually include
the manner of death.

Marmalade

He's buried in the bushes,
with dockleaves round his grave,
A crimecat desperado
and his name was Marmalade.
He's the cat that caught the pigeon,
that stole the neighbour's meat . . .
and tore the velvet curtains
and stained the satin seat.
He's the cat that spoilt the laundry,
he's the cat that spilt the stew,
and chased the lady's poodle
and scratched her daughter too.

But –
No more we'll hear his cat flap,
or scratches at the door,
or see him at the window,
or hear his catnap snore.
So –
Ring his grave with pebbles,
erect a noble sign –
For here lies Marmalade
and Marmalade was MINE.

Peter Dixon

Epitaph for the Last Martian

Crash landing caused extinction
The last of the Martian species
Here and here and here and here
He rests in pieces.

Paul Cookson

Dead End

In memory of Charlotte Cul-de-sac,
A loyal and trusted friend.
She finally lived up to her name
And came to a dead end.

John Foster

My Thin Friend

Here lies the body
Of stick insect Fred
He didn't move for three whole days
I hope he *was* dead.

Roger Stevens

In Memoriam

Beneath this stone
lies
ALBERT GRIST
who will not
be sadly missed.
We have lost
a bore, a pain,
but our loss
is
Heaven's gain!

Sue Cowling

An Epitaph

Here lies a most beautiful lady,
Light of step and heart was she;
I think she was the most beautiful lady
That ever was in the West Country.

But beauty vanishes; beauty passes;
However rare – rare it be;
And when I crumble, who will remember
This lady of the West Country?

Walter de la Mare

303

She Dwelt Among the Untrodden Ways

She dwelt among the untrodden ways
    Beside the springs of Dove,
A Maid whom there were none to praise
    And very few to love:

A violet by a mossy stone
    Half-hidden from the eye!
— Fair as a star, when only one
    Is shining in the sky.

She lived unknown, and few could know
    When Lucy ceased to be;
But she is in her grave, and, oh,
    The difference to me!

                William Wordsworth

Epitaph for a Gifted Man

He was not known among his friends for wit;
He owned no wealth, nor did he crave for it.
His looks would never draw a second glance;
He could not play an instrument or dance,
Or sing, or paint, nor would he ever write
The music, plays, or poems that delight
And win the whole world's worship and applause.
He did not fight for any noble cause;
Showed neither great extravagance nor thrift;
But he loved greatly: that was his one gift.

Vernon Scannell

For Johnny

Do not despair
For Johnny-head-in-air;
He sleeps as sound
As Johnny under ground.

Fetch out no shroud
For Johnny-in-the-cloud;
And keep your tears
For him in after years.

Better by far
For Johnny-the-bright-star,
To keep your head,
And see his children fed.

John Pudney

In 1905, Catherine Alsopp, a Sheffield washerwoman, composed her own epitaph before hanging herself.

Here lies a poor woman who always was tired;
She lived in a house where help was not hired,
Her last words on earth were: 'Dear friends, I am going
Where washing ain't done, nor sweeping, nor sewing.
But everything there is exact to my wishes,
For where they don't eat, there's no washing of dishes
I'll be where loud anthems will always be ringing
But having no voice, I'll be clear of the singing.
Don't mourn for me now, don't mourn for me never,
I'm going to do nothing for ever and ever.'

Catherine Alsopp

Elegies

A poem or song which is a lament for someone
or something that has passed away or is no longer around.

It's Not the Same Any More

It's not the same since Patch died.
Sticks are sticks.
Never thrown, never fetched.

It's not the same any more.
Tennis balls lie still and lifeless.
The urge to bounce them has gone.

It's not the same now.
I can't bring myself to whistle.
There's no reason to do so.

His collar hangs on the hook
and his name tag and lead are dusty.

His basket and bowl are in a plastic bag
lying at an angle on a garage shelf.

My new slippers will never be chewed
and I've no excuse for my lack of homework any more.

I can now watch the football in peace, uninterrupted.
No frantic barking and leaping just when it gets to the goal.

I don't have to share my sweets and biscuits
and then wipe the dribbling drool off my trouser legs.

It's just not the same any more.
When Patch died a small part of me died too.

All that's left is a mound of earth
and my hand-made cross beneath the apple tree.

All that's left are the memories.
Thousands of them.

It's just not the same any more.

Paul Cookson

Future Past

Lord of Africa,
swaying giant of the plains;
tree-mover,
sand-tosser,
diviner of water
from the dry river bed:
where are you now?

Where is the song on ivory keys
that echoed through the dusk?
The song's cut away
for a handful of beads
which once were a living tusk.
Now only baubles
glint in the sun,
for the forest lord fell
to the sound of a gun.

Judith Nicholls

For My Mother

I   My Mother Dying Aged 87

You died as quietly as your spirit moved
All through my life. It was a shock to hear
Your shallow breathing and more hard to see
Your eyes closed fast. You did not wake for me
But even so I do not shed a tear.
Your spirit has flown free

Of that small shell of flesh. Grandchildren stood
Quietly by and it was they who gave
Most strength to us. They also loved you for
Your gentleness. You never made them fear
Anything. The memories you leave
Are happy times. You were

The one who gave me stamps and envelopes
And posted all my early poems. You had
Such faith in me. You could be firm and would
Curb tantrums, and would change an angry mood
With careful threats. I cannot feel too sad
Today for you were good

And that is what the kindly letters say.
Some are clumsy, some embarrass with
Lush piety but all will guide your ship
Upon a calm, bright ocean and we keep
Our eyes on it. It is too strong for death
And so we do not weep.

II   *Grief*

I miss my mother today.
I went into a shop and saw the Mothering Sunday
Cards in bright array.
I always used to send her one and now
There is nothing to write or say.

Grief can strike you when
You least expect it. It's an emptiness
Easy to fill with pain.
My mother had no rage, was always kind.
When will she come again

And darken and haunt the large room of my mind?

Elizabeth Jennings

Poem for a Dead Poet

He was a poet he was.
A proper poet.
He said things
that made you think
and said them nicely.
He saw things
that you or I
could never see
and saw them clearly.
He had a way
with language.
Images flocked around
him like birds,
St Francis, he was,
of the words. Words?
Why he could almost make 'em talk.

Roger McGough

Cat's Funeral

Bury her deep, down deep,
Safe in the earth's cold keep,
Bury her deep –

No more to watch bird stir;
No more to clean dark fur;
No more to glisten as silk;
No more to revel in milk;
No more to purr.

Bury her deep, down deep;
She is beyond warm sleep.
She will not walk in the night;
She will not wake to the light.
Bury her deep.

E.V. Rieu

Nonsense Poems

These are poems that use fantasies, make up their own language and their own worlds. Often they contradict themselves – *One fine day in the middle of the night.* Sometimes they just don't make any sense at all – hence the term 'nonsense poetry'.

Jabberwocky

'Twas brillig, and the slithy toves
   Did gyre and gimble in the wabe;
All mimsy were the borogoves,
     And the mome raths outgrabe.

'Beware the Jabberwock, my son!
   The jaws that bite, the claws that catch!
Beware the Jubjub bird, and shun
     The frumious Bandersnatch!'

He took his vorpal sword in hand:
   Long time the manxome foe he sought –
So rested he by the Tumtum tree,
     And stood awhile in thought.

And as in uffish thought he stood,
   The Jabberwock, with eyes of flame,
Came whiffling through the tulgey wood,
     And burbled as it came!

One, two! One, two! And through and through
   The vorpal blade went snicker-snack!
He left it dead, and with its head
     He went galumphing back.

'And hast thou slain the Jabberwock?
    Come to my arms, my beamish boy!
O frabjous day! Callooh! Callay!'
    He chortled in his joy.

'Twas brillig, and the slithy toves
    Did gyre and gimble in the wabe;
All mimsy were the borogoves,
        And the mome raths outgrabe.

Lewis Carroll

Jabbermockery

'Twas Thursday and the naughty girls
Did gyre and gimble in the gym.
All mimsy was Miss Borogrove
And Mr Maths was grim.

'Beware the Number Man, my friend!
His sums that snarl. His co-ordinates that catch!
Beware the Deputy Bird, and shun
The evil Earring-snatch!'

She took her ballpoint pen in hand:
Long time the problem's end she sought –
So rested she by the lavatory
And sat awhile in thought.

And as in toughish thought she sat,
The Number Man with eyes of flame
Came calculating through the cloakroom doors
And subtracted as he came.

She thought real fast as he went past;
The well-placed soap went slickersmack!
She left him stunned and with the sums
She went galumphing back.

'And has thou got the answers, Jackie?
Come to our desk,' beamed idle boys.
'Oh, frabjous day, Quelle heure! Calais!'
They chortled in their joy.

'Twas Thursday and the naughty girls
Did gyre and gimble in the gym.
All mimsy was Miss Borogrove
And Mr Maths was grim.

Trevor Millum

Before the Days of Noah

Before the days of Noah
before he built his ark
seagulls sang like nightingales
and lions sang like larks.
The tortoise had a mighty roar
the cockerel had a moo
kitten always eeyored
and elephants just mewed
    It was the way the world was
    . . . when owls had a bark
    and dogs did awful crowings
    whilst running round the park.
Horses baaaed like baa lambs
ducks could all miaow
and animals had voices
quite different from now!
But, came the day of flooding
and all the world was dark
the animals got weary
of living in the ark –
    So they swapped around their voices
    a trumpet for a mew
    – a silly sort of pastime
    when nothing much to do.
But when the flood had ended
and the world was nice and dry
the creatures had forgotten
how once they hissed or cried.

So they kept their brand-new voices
   – forgot the days before
   – when lions used to giggle
   and gerbils used to roar.

Peter Dixon

Night Mer

One night when I was fast apeels
all duggled snown and warm
I had a very dasty ream
about a stunder thorm
and fightning lashed
and saves at wea
like boilings werpents sithed
and foaming angs did frockle me
and shicked and slucked and eyethed.
They ulled me under, lungings full
of fevvered, fluffin fug
till suffing grably I apized
upon the redboom bug.

Gina Douthwaite

Fantastic Facts

Farmers
In the Bahamas
Seldom wear pyjamas

Police
In Greece
Often keep geese

The rain
In Spain
Sometimes travels by train

Most people in Cuba
Know how to scuba
But nobody plays the tuba

The well-to-do
In Peru
Always wear blue

No one wears a tie
In Paraguay
(Don't ask me why)

In Japan
A man
Isn't expected to carry a fan

The staff in hotels
In the Seychelles
Like ringing bells

In Mauritius
The food is delicious
And quite nutritious

The moon
In Cameroon
Rises at noon.

John Irwin

The Jumblies

[I]

They went to sea in a Sieve, they did,
  In a Sieve they went to sea:
In spite of all their friends could say,
On a winter's morn, on a stormy day,
  In a Sieve they went to sea!
And when the Sieve turned round and round,
And every one cried, 'You'll all be drowned!'
They called aloud, 'Our Sieve ain't big,
But we don't care a button! we don't care a fig!
  In a Sieve we'll go to sea!'
    Far and few, far and few,
      Are the lands where the Jumblies live
Their heads are green, and their hands are blue
      And they went to sea in a Sieve.

[II]

They sailed in a Sieve, they did,
  In a Sieve, they sailed so fast,
With only a beautiful pea-green veil
Tied with a riband by way of a sail,
    To a small tobacco-pipe mast;
And every one said, who saw them go,
'O won't they be soon upset, you know!
For the sky is dark, and the voyage is long,
And happen what may, it's extremely wrong
  In a Sieve to sail so fast!'
    Far and few, far and few,
      Are the lands where the Jumblies live;
Their heads are green, and their hands are blue,
      And they went to sea in a Sieve.

[III]

The water it soon came in, it did,
  The water it soon came in;
So to keep them dry, they wrapped their feet
In a pinky paper all folded neat,
  And they fastened it down with a pin.
And they passed the night in a crockery-jar,
And each of them said, 'How wise we are!
Though the sky be dark, and the voyage be long,
Yet we never can think we were rash or wrong,
  While round in our Sieve we spin!'
    Far and few, far and few,
      Are the lands where the Jumblies live;
Their heads are green, and their hands are blue,
      And they went to sea in a Sieve.

[IV]

And all night long they sailed away;
   And when the sun went down,
They whistled and warbled a moony song
To the echoing sound of a coppery gong,
   In the shade of the mountains brown.
'O Timballo! How happy we are,
When we live in a sieve and a crockery-jar,
And all night long in the moonlight pale,
We sail away with a pea-green sail,
   In the shade of the mountains brown!'
    Far and few, far and few,
      Are the lands where the Jumblies live;
Their heads are green, and their hands are blue,
     And they went to sea in a Sieve.

Edward Lear

I Went to the Pictures Tomorrow

I went to the pictures tomorrow
I took a front seat at the back,
I fell from the pit to the gallery
And broke a front bone in my back.
A lady she gave me some chocolate,
I ate it and gave it her back.
I phoned for a taxi and walked it,
And that's why I never came back.

Anon.

When I Went Out for a Walk One Day

When I went out for a walk one day,
My head fell off and rolled away,
And when I saw that it was gone –
I picked it up and put it on.

When I went into the street
Someone shouted, 'Look at your feet!'
I looked at them and sadly said,
'I've left them both asleep in bed!'

Anon.

330

On the Ning Nang Nong

On the Ning Nang Nong
Where the Cows go Bong!
And the Monkeys all say Boo!
There's a Nong Nang Ning
Where the trees go Ping!
And the teapots Jibber Jabber Joo.
On the Nong Ning Nang
All the mice go Clang!
And you just can't catch 'em when they do!
So it's Ning Nang Nong!
Cows go Bong!
Nong Nang Ning!
Trees go Ping!
Nong Ning Nang!
The mice go Clang!
What a noisy place to belong,
Is the Ning Nang Ning Nang Nong!!

Spike Milligan

'Quack!' Said the Billy-goat

'Quack!' said the billy-goat.
'Oink!' said the hen.
'Miaow!' said the little chick
Running in the pen.

'Hobble-gobble!' said the dog.
'Cluck!' said the sow.
'Tu-whit tu-whoo!' the donkey said.
'Baa!' said the cow.

'Hee-haw!' the turkey cried.
The duck began to moo.
All at once the sheep went,
'Cock-a-doodle-doo!'

The owl coughed and cleared his throat
And he began to bleat
'Bow-wow!' said the cock
Swimming in the leat.

'Cheep-cheep!' said the cat
As she began to fly.
'Farmer's been and laid an egg –
That's the reason why.'

Charles Causley

Adverts/Jingles

Verses and lines used to draw attention to a product and thereby make it memorable. Often they use lots of alliteration, repetition and rhyme to make them as catchy as possible.

The Caractacus Chariot Company

FOR SALE:
SECOND-HAND WAR CHARIOT

One Careful Owner (rumoured to be
Queen Boudicca of the Iceni)
Low Mileage
Two or Four Horsepower
Wheels with Sharp Knives (if required)
5 months Woad Tax
Blood-Red Bodywork
inlaid with **Roman Bones**

Has taken part in several
Successful Battles:

> the **Sacking** of **Camulodunum**
> **Attacks on Londonium**
> Many Minor Skirmishes

Backed by our **First Class Druid Warranty**

Must be seen to be believed!
Only **3 gold pieces** o.n.o.

Will **Exchange** for quantity
of belts, buckles and bronze shields.

Don't delay, view today, at
THE CARACTACUS CHARIOT COMPANY™

Mike Johnson

Poem for Sale

Poem For Sale
(One careful owner)
With simile
(as lucky as a dime),
Two exquisite
And erudite adjectives
And one rhyme

Going
For a song.

Roger Stevens

Trainee Witch Wanted

WANTED!

One trainee witch,
not very old,
with a nasty laugh
but a heart of gold.

With pointy nails,
who wouldn't hurt a flea,
just to stir the pot
of the witches' tea.

Andrew Collett

Career Opportunity: Knight Required

Are you courageous, honourable
and chivalrous?
Do you enjoy wearing metal suits
and enjoy being called Sir?
Then this could be the job for you.

Your duties will include
wielding a sword, jousting
and clanking about.

Preference will be given
to those candidates
who come equipped
with their own warhorse and squire.

If you think
you've got what it takes
turn up for an interview
and show us what you can do.

NB Candidates will be left
to fight it out amongst themselves.
Castle Management accepts no responsibility
for loss of life or limb.

Bernard Young

My Mum's Put Me on the Transfer List

On Offer:
one nippy striker, ten years old
has scored seven goals this season
has nifty footwork and a big smile
knows how to dive in the penalty box
can get filthy and muddy within two minutes
guaranteed to wreck his kit each week
this is a FREE TRANSFER
but he comes with running expenses:
weeks of washing shirts and shorts
socks and vests, a pair of trainers
needs to scoff huge amounts
of chips and burgers, beans and apples
pop and cola, crisps and oranges
endless packets of chewing gum.
This offer open until the end of the season
I'll have him back then
at least until the cricket starts.
Any takers?

David Harmer

Letters

Poems that take the form of letters. They may use rhyme, they may not.

Dear Mum

While you were out
A cup went and broke itself on purpose.
A crack appeared in that old blue vase your great granddad
Got from Mr Ming.
Somehow without me even turning on the tap
The sink mysteriously overflowed.
A strange jam-stain, about the size of my hand,
Suddenly appeared on the kitchen wall.
I don't think we'll ever discover exactly how the cat
Managed to turn on the washing machine
(Specially from the inside)
Or how Sis's pet rabbit went and mistook
The waste-disposal unit for a burrow.
I can tell you, I was really scared when, as if by magic,
A series of muddy footprints appeared on your new white
    carpet.
Also, I know the canary looks grubby,
But it took ages and ages
Getting it out the vacuum-cleaner
I was being good (honest)
But I think the house is haunted so,
Knowing you're going to have a fit,
I've gone over to Gran's to lie low for a bit.

Brian Patten

Letter to my Uncle

1912. The 17th of March.

Dear Uncle,

Thank you for your invitation to sail with you next month. I'd very much like to accept but there's a complication – I really ought to write and ask my parents. They may not let me miss more time from school after my illness. So, with your forbearance, I'll write. But stopping me would be too cruel!

I hear that the *Titanic*'s really something – the biggest thing afloat, that's what they say. Her maiden voyage! And I could be coming. If they say no, I think I'll stow away! Perhaps there's hope though. Maybe they'll agree. I'll let you know.

Your loving nephew,

G

Jill Townsend

The Ancient Order of Insects
Beetle Drive
Antrim

Dear Mrs Spider,

Your application form has come to my attention
but it raises issues that I need to mention.
Apparently you have eight legs
Which is two too many
And when asked to fill in 'Type of wings.'
You declared that you hadn't any.
You say your body is in only two parts
when the required number is three;
You call your home a web
and like to eat flies for tea.

Therefore, I am afraid that I must reject
Your request to become AN INSECT.

Yours truly,

The Chief Bluebottle
(Membership Secretary)

John Coldwell

Thank You Letters

Dear Mr Thomas Smith,
Thank you for your crackers.
What a splendid novelty –
They really made our day!

Dear Your Royal Highness,
Thank you for the Christmas tree.
A most original idea
Of yours, if I may say!

My dear Sir Henry Cole,
Thank you for the Christmas card.
Your very own invention
And an excellent one too!

Dear Mr Rowland Hill,
Thank you for the postage stamp.
A good try, but I don't believe
It will catch on, do you?

Sue Cowling

Absent

Dear Teacher,
my body's arrived
it sits at a table
a pen in its hand
as if it is able
to think and to act
perhaps write down the answer
to the question you've asked

but don't let that fool you.

My mind is elsewhere.
My thoughts far away.

So apologies, teacher,
I'm not here today.

Bernard Young

Postcard from School Camp

*D*ear Mum and Dad,

   Weather's poor, food's bad, teachers are grumpy, instructors are mad. Cramped in tent, cold at night, no dry clothes, boots too tight. Didn't like canoeing, the hiking was tough, all in all I've had enough.
  Bye for now, MAY see you soon
   If I survive this afternoon
    Your loving son,
    Ben xx

P.S. Can I come again next year?

         Richard Caley

Letter to an Unknown Father

Dear Father,
                I have never seen you.
                I do not know your name,
                I've no idea where you live
                Or whose should be the blame.

                I wonder what you look like?
                Maybe you look like me?
                When I look in morning mirrors
                Is yours the face I see?

                Will I ever get to know you
                Before the clock runs down?
                How I wonder as I wander
                Through all the tired town.

                Although I've never known you,
                I miss you all the same.
                I wonder if you're sad like me
                At this broken family game?

                I hope one day to meet you
                Before our race is run.
                I think of you just every day.

                    Your puzzled, loving son.

                        John Kitching

Bee! I'm Expecting You!

Bee! I'm expecting you!
Was saying yesterday
To somebody you know
That you were due.

The frogs got home last week,
Are settled, and at work;
Birds, mostly back,
To clover warm and thick.

You'll get my letter by
the seventeenth; reply
Or better, be with me,
Yours, Fly.

Emily Dickinson

From a Problem Page

Dear Maureen,
I am a lamp-post.
Every Saturday evening at five o'clock
three boys
wearing blue and white scarves
blue and white hats
waving their arms in the air
and shouting,
come my way.
Sometimes they kick me.
Sometimes they kiss me.
What should I do
to get them to make up their minds?
Yours bewilderedly,
Annie Onlight.

Michael Rosen

A Superhero Sends a Letter Home

Dear Mum,
Things haven't been too good just lately
Speeding bullets overtake me
My dizzy spells and fear of heights
Inconvenience all my flights.
The purple tights you sent at last
Have given me a nasty rash.
X-ray vision's not all it seems
I'm sick of seeing bones and spleens.
My tinnitus is getting worse
The seams upon my trunks have burst.
I've got an aching in my head
I'm out of breath getting out of bed
To top it all the yoghurt stains
In my satin cloak remain.
My love life hit a downward whirl
I'm no longer seeing Dandruff Girl.
She's gone off with Ali Tosis
The Bad Breath Boy who smells the mostest.
I'm scared of going out at night
I run away when I should fight.
So as you see things could be better
But not much worse as I end this letter.
My super powers are minus zero
Your loving son,

A Failing Hero
XXXX
Paul Cookson

352

William the Conqueror Sends
a Postcard Home

Hastings 14th Oct 1066

Dear Mum,

Having a lovely time in England.
Arrived at Pevensey but the beach was rubbish.
Moved to Battle – and guess what?
Had a battle there (ho ho)
Harold turned up late (typically British)
So we chose to defend the hill (clever move)
Not much luck with horses (three killed!)
Men needed to know I was alive, so
Fought without helmet.
(I know I promised to wear it all the time)
We pretended to run away (very clever)
The English chased us (very stupid)
Result – One nil to the Normans.
Guess what? I have a new nickname.
William the Conqueror (good eh?)
Weather fine . . . Wish you were here.
Your loving son,
William (King of England!)
P.S. England is now back to Norman (ho! ho! ho!)

John Coldwell

Diaries

Poems that take the form of a diary, noting special events and occasions. They often show the passing of time, for example, *My Busy Week As A Pop Star*, or could even be *My Busy Day As A Pop Star*, and would give some sort of insight into the character writing them.

Football Training

Monday
Practised heading the ball:
Missed it – nutted the neighbours' wall.

Tuesday
Perfected my sideline throw:
Fell in the mud – forgot to let go!

Wednesday
Worked on my penalty kick:
A real bruiser – my toe met a brick.

Thursday
Gained stamina – went for a jog:
Ran round in circles – lost in the fog!

Friday
Developed my tactical play:
Tackled the goal post – it got in the way.

Saturday
Exercised – twenty-eight press-ups:
Did pull a muscle – but no major mess-ups.

Sunday
At last – the day of the match!
Came through it all without a scratch.
The ref was amazed how I kept my nerve;
He agreed it's not easy to be the reserve!

Celia Warren

Victorian Diarist

My name is Ebenezer Gray.
I wear my top hat every day,
but take it off to go to bed
and put my nightcap on instead.
Before I sleep I always write,
in Indian ink by candlelight,
neat notes nibbed in copperplate
on what I've known and done that date.

It's the diary of Ebenezer Gray
who wore his top hat all that day
and, though each day is much the same,
he fills its page, then snuffs the flame.
And downstairs in the darkened hall,
the tall clock stands, with back to wall.
It ticks and tuts, solemnly dour,
and all night chimes to mark the hour.

Undreaming, Ebenezer Gray,
who'll wear his top hat all today,
is roused by maid with morning meal.
Outside, the sounds of hoof and wheel.
Now nearer noises fill his room
of shovelled coal and driven broom;
while waking smells of baking bread
give way to polish, soaps, blacklead.

Good morning, Ebenezer Gray!
Your top hat's there again today.
You're trimmed and tailored, looking fine,
stiff collar upright, like your spine.
You've breakfasted on bread and kippers.
You've read *The Times* in gown and slippers.
Now groomed and dressed with waxed moustache
you're dapper, without being flash.

Yes, I am Ebenezer Gray.
I wear this top hat every day.
I pause to raise it when I meet
an old acquaintance in the street.
We nod and smile to be polite
though conversation wouldn't be right.
Besides, I very seldom speak
save once or maybe twice a week.

So there goes Ebenezer Gray,
top-hatted for another day.
Across the park with walking cane
he strides to horse-drawn tram or train.
At five-fifteen, he's home again,
his life a pattern he'll maintain
till death comes knocking on his door
in the spring of 1894.

Nick Toczek

Julius Caesar

Entry for March 15th

Dear Diary,
I'm tired this morning.
Didn't feel like breakfast
Hardly touched the olives, lark or dormouse
We stayed out late last night
With Lepidus
And talked of immortality
Drank too much wine
And now Calpurnia, my wife,
Is in a mood
Last night she dreamed of death
And it was mine

I'm tired this morning
The winds of March
blow like a hurricane
around the seven hills.
At the Pontifical Palace
The God of Mars crashed to the floor
But what that means I'm not quite sure

I'm tired this morning
On this, the Ides of March,
I'm tired of ruling Rome
And so, dear Diary,
The Senate can convene without me
And today I'll stay at home.

(On the morning of Julius Caesar's assassination, the chamber at the Senate was full. But Caesar's chair was empty. He was nowhere to be found. The conspirators sent Marcus Brutus to Caesar's house to persuade him to attend.)

Translated from the Latin by Roger Stevens

The First Diary

Day 1:   Darkandlightday.
Day 2:   Seaandskyday.
Day 3:   Earthgrassandtreegotaweebitcarriedawayday!
Day 4:   Sunmoonandstarsday.
Day 5:   Fishandbirdday.
Day 6:   Manandbeastday.
Day 7:   ThinkI'llcallitadayday!

Sue Cowling

A Day in the Life of Danny the Cat

Danny wakcs up
Eats
Finds a private place in the garden,
He returns
Plays with the plants
And sleeps.
Danny wakes up
Eats
Inspects the garden
Finds a cosy place
And sleeps.
Danny wakes up
Comes indoors
Inspects the carpet

Scratches himself
And sleeps.
Danny wakes up
Goes in the garden
Over the fence
Has a fight with Ginger
Makes a date with Sandy
Climbs on to next door's shed
And sleeps.
Danny wakes up
Comes indoors
Rubs up the chair leg
Rubs up a human leg
Sharpens his claws
On a human leg
Eats
And sleeps.
Danny wakes up
Eats
Watches a nature programme
Finds a private place in the garden,
Finds Sandy in next door's garden
Next door's dog finds Danny
Sandy runs north
Danny runs home
Eats and sleeps.
Danny wakes up
Checks for mice
Checks for birds
Checks for dogs

Checks for food
Finds a private place in the garden
Eats
And sleeps.
Danny has hobbies,
Being stroked
Car-watching
And smelling feet
He loves life,
Keeps fit
And keeps clean,
Every night he covers himself
In spit,
Then he eats
And sleeps.

Benjamin Zephaniah

Couplets

These are poems that have two consecutive lines of rhyme
– usually the same length and same rhythm.

Kicking Up Leaves

Crunching,
Scrunching,

Scattering,
Shattering,

Brown ones,
Gold ones,

Crispy,
Wispy,

Scuttery,
Fluttery,

Skittery,
Flittery,

Scuffly,
Luffly!!

Matt Simpson

The Witches' School of Flying

'To fly your broomstick, take one cat
then place on head your witch's hat.
Put cat on stick towards the end,
jump on, sit straight; you shouldn't bend.'
Thus instructed Mistress Dale
to Arabella Nightingale
who wore an L-plate painted red,
a brand-new hat upon her head,
and carried, with a muffled groan,
a cat, who weighed at least two stone.
The broomstick quivered – took off fast.
The treetops swayed as they zoomed past.
Then, flying high above the crowd,
they somersaulted through a cloud.
The trainee witch was heard to wail,
'Too much weight upon the tail.'
The cat, with his enormous girth,
fell off and spiralled down to earth.
But Arabella cast a spell,
and in a second, all was well.
The watching witches yelled, 'How cute,
he's got a magic parachute.'
Then Arabella landed – SPLAT –
in time to catch her floating cat.
The witch instructress muttered, 'Phew!!
Report next week for lesson two.'

Marian Swinger

The Tyger

Tyger! Tyger! burning bright
In the forests of the night,
What immortal hand or eye
Could frame thy fearful symmetry?

In what distant deeps or skies
Burnt the fire of thine eyes?
On what wings dare he aspire?
What the hand dare seize the fire?

And what shoulder, and what art,
Could twist the sinews of thy heart?
And when thy heart began to beat,
What dread hand? and what dread feet?

What the hammer? what the chain?
In what furnace was thy brain?
What the anvil? what dread grasp
Dare its deadly terrors clasp?

When the stars threw down their spears,
And water'd heaven with their tears,
Did he smile his work to see?
Did he who made the Lamb make thee?

Tyger! Tyger! burning bright
In the forests of the night,
What immortal hand or eye
Dare frame thy fearful symmetry?

William Blake

Matilda

who told lies, and was burned to death

Matilda told such Dreadful Lies,
It made one Gasp and Stretch one's Eyes;
Her Aunt, who, from her Earliest Youth,
Had kept a Strict Regard for Truth,
Attempted to Believe Matilda:
The effort very nearly killed her,
And would have done so, had not She
Discovered this Infirmity.
For once, towards the Close of Day,
Matilda, growing tired of play,
And finding she was left alone,
Went tiptoe to the Telephone
And summoned the Immediate Aid
Of London's Noble Fire-Brigade.
Within an hour the Gallant Band
Were pouring in on every hand,
From Putney, Hackney Downs and Bow,

With Courage High, and Hearts aglow,
They galloped, roaring through the Town,
'Matilda's House is Burning Down!'
Inspired by British Cheers and Loud
Proceeding from the Frenzied Crowd,
They ran their ladders through a score
Of windows on the Ball Room Floor;
And took Peculiar Pains to Souse
The Pictures up and down the house,
Until Matilda's Aunt succeeded
In showing them they were not needed
And even then she had to pay
To get the Men to go away!

It happened that a few Weeks later
Her Aunt was off to the Theatre
To see that interesting Play
The Second Mrs Tanqueray.
She had refused to take her Niece
To hear this Entertaining Piece:
A Deprivation Just and Wise
To Punish her for Telling Lies.
That Night a Fire *did* break out –
You should have heard Matilda Shout!
You should have heard her Scream and Bawl,
And throw the window up and call
To People passing in the Street –
(The rapidly increasing Heat
Encouraging her to obtain
Their confidence) – but all in vain!

For every time She shouted 'Fire!'
They only answered 'Little Liar!'
And therefore when her Aunt returned,
Matilda, and the House, were Burned.

Hilaire Belloc

Fire, Burn; and Cauldron, Bubble

Round about the cauldron go;
In the poison'd entrails throw.
Toad, that under cold stone
Days and nights has thirty-one
Swelter'd venom, sleeping got,
Boil thou first i'th'charmed pot.
Double, double toil and trouble:
Fire, burn; and cauldron, bubble.
Fillet of a fenny snake,
In the cauldron boil and bake;
Eye of newt, and toe of frog,
Wool of bat, and tongue of dog,
Adder's fork, and blind-worm's sting,
Lizard's leg, and howlet's wing.
For a charm of powerful trouble,
Like a hell-broth boil and bubble.
Double, double toil and trouble:
Fire, burn; and cauldron, bubble.

William Shakespeare

Who is de Girl?

Who is de girl dat kick de ball
then jump for it over de wall

sallyann is a girl so full-o zest
sallyann is a girl dat just can't rest

who is de girl dat pull de hair
of de bully and make him scare

sallyann is a girl so full-o zest
sallyann is a girl dat just can't rest

who is de girl dat bruise she knee
when she fall from de mango tree

sallyann is a girl so full-o zest
sallyann is a girl dat just can't rest

who is de girl dat set de pace
when boys and girls dem start to race

sallyann is a girl so full-o zest
sallyann is a girl dat just can't rest.

John Agard

My Brother Bert

Pets are the Hobby of my brother Bert.
He used to go to school with a Mouse in his shirt.

His Hobby it grew, as some hobbies will,
And grew and GREW and GREW until –

Oh don't breathe a word, pretend you haven't heard.
A simply appalling thing has occurred –

The very thought makes me iller and iller:
Bert's brought home a gigantic Gorilla!

If you think that's really not such a scare,
What if it quarrels with his Grizzly Bear?

You still think you could keep your head?
What if the Lion from under the bed

And the four Ostriches that deposit
Their football eggs in his bedroom closet

And the Aardvark out of his bottom drawer
All danced out and joined in the Roar?

What if the Pangolins were to caper
Out of their nests behind the wallpaper?

With the fifty sorts of Bats
That hang on his hatstand like old hats,

And out of a shoebox the excitable Platypus
Along with the Ocelot or Jungle-Cattypus?

The Wombat, the Dingo, the Gecko, the Grampus –
How they would shake the house with their Rumpus!

Not to forget the Bandicoot
Who would certainly peer from his battered old boot.

Why it could be a dreadful day,
And what Oh what would the neighbours say!

Ted Hughes

The Bonfire

This cloud of smoke in other hours
Was leaves and grass, green twigs and flowers.

This bitter-sweet dead smell that blows
Was once the breathing of the rose.

Shapeless the forms of petals fair
And slender leaves melt on the air,

And in a scent she never knew
In life, the rose departeth too.

Eleanor Farjeon

Songs

Poems that have a rhythmic even structure that enable them to be sung. They usually rhyme and sometimes involve a chorus. They may tell stories or be in praise of something. Ballads are often songs.

A Morning Song
For the First Day of Spring

Morning has broken
Like the first morning,
Blackbird has spoken
    Like the first bird.
Praise for the singing!
Praise for the morning!
Praise for them, springing
    From the first Word.

Sweet the rain's new fall
Sunlit from heaven,
Like the first dewfall
    In the first hour.
Praise for the sweetness
Of the wet garden,
Sprung in completeness
    From the first shower.

Mine is the sunlight!
Mine is the morning
Born of the one light
    Eden saw play.
Praise with elation,
Praise every morning
Spring's re-creation
    Of the First Day!

Eleanor Farjeon

Jerusalem

And did those feet in ancient time
　　Walk upon England's mountains green?
And was the holy Lamb of God
　　On England's pleasant pasture seen?

And did the Countenance Divine
　　Shine forth upon our clouded hills?
And was Jerusalem builded here
　　Among these dark Satanic Mills?

Bring me my bow of burning gold!
　　Bring me my arrows of desire!
Bring me my spear! O clouds, unfold!
　　Bring me my chariot of fire!

I will not cease from mental fight,
　　Nor shall my sword sleep in my hand,
Till we have built Jerusalem
　　In England's green and pleasant land.

William Blake

Waltzing Matilda

Oh! there once was a swagman camped by a Billabong
Under the shade of a Coolabah tree;
And he sang as he looked at his old billy boiling,
'Who'll come a-waltzing Matilda with me?'

Who'll come a-waltzing Matilda, my darling,
Who'll come a-waltzing Matilda with me?
Waltzing Matilda and leading a water-bag –
Who'll come a-waltzing Matilda with me?

Down came a jumbuck to drink at the water-hole,
Up jumped the swagman and grabbed him in glee;
And he sang as he stowed him away in his tucker-bag,
'You'll come a-waltzing Matilda with me!'

Down came the Squatter a-riding his thoroughbred;
Down came Policemen – one, two, and three.
'Who is the jumbuck you've got in the tucker-bag?
You'll come a-waltzing Matilda with me.'

But the swagman, he up and he jumped in the water-hole,
Drowning himself by the Coolabah tree;
And his ghost may be heard as it sings in the Billabong,
'Who'll come a-waltzing Matilda with me?'

A. B. (Banjo) Paterson

A Smuggler's Song

If you wake at midnight and hear a horse's feet,
Don't go drawing back the blind, or looking in the street,

Them that asks no questions isn't told a lie.
Watch the wall, my darling, while the Gentlemen go by!
   Five and twenty ponies,
   Trotting through the dark –
   Brandy for the Parson,
   Baccy for the Clerk;
   Laces for a lady; letters for a spy,
And watch the wall, my darling, while the Gentlemen go by!

Running round the woodlump if you chance to find
Little barrels, roped and tarred, all full of brandy-wine;
Don't you shout to come and look, nor take 'em for your
   play;
Put the brushwood back again, – and they'll be gone next
   day!

If you see the stableyard setting open wide;
If you see a tired horse lying down inside;
If your mother mends a coat cut about and tore;
If the lining's wet and warm – don't you ask no more!

If you meet King George's men, dressed in blue and red,
You be careful what you say, and mindful what is said.
If they call you 'pretty maid', and chuck you 'neath the chin,
Don't you tell where no one is, nor yet where no one's been!

Knocks and footsteps round the house – whistles after
   dark –
You've no call for running out till the housedogs bark.
Trusty's here and Pincher's here, and see how dumb they
   lie –
They don't fret to follow when the Gentlemen go by!

If you do as you've been told, likely there's a chance,
You'll be given a dainty dolly, – all the way from France,
With a cap of Valenciennes, and a velvet hood –
A present from the Gentlemen, along o' being good!
   Five and twenty ponies,
   Trotting through the dark –
   Brandy for the Parson,
   Baccy for the Clerk;
Them that asks no questions isn't told a lie –
Watch the wall, my darling, while the Gentlemen go by!

Rudyard Kipling

The Song of the Mischievous Dog

There are many who say that a dog has its day,
And a cat has a number of lives;
There are others who think that a lobster is pink,
And that bees never work in their hives.
There are fewer, of course, who insist that a horse
Has a horn and two humps on its head,
And a fellow who jests that a mare can build nests
Is as rare as a donkey that's red.
Yet in spite of all this, I have moments of bliss,
For I cherish a passion for bones,
And though doubtful of biscuit, I'm willing to risk it,
And I love to chase rabbits and stones.
But my greatest delight is to take a good bite
At a calf that is plump and delicious;
And if I indulge in a bite at a bulge,
Let's hope you won't think me too vicious.

Dylan Thomas

Auld Lang Syne

Should auld acquaintance be forgot,
And never brought to min'?
Should auld acquaintance be forgot,
And auld lang syne?

For auld lang syne, my dear.
For auld lang syne,
We'll tak a cup o' kindness yet,
For auld lang syne.

We twa hae run about the braes,
And pu'd the gowans fine;
But we've wandered mony a weary foot
Sin' auld lang syne.
We twa hae paidled i' the burn,
From morning sun till dine;
But seas between us braid hae roared
Sin' auld lang syne.

And there's a hand, my trusty fiere,
And gie's a hand o' thine;
And we'll tak a right guid-willie waught,
For auld lang syne.

And surely ye'll be your pint-stowp,
And surely I'll be mine;
And we'll tak a cup o' kindness yet
For auld lang syne.

For auld lang syne, my dear.
For auld lang syne,
We'll tak a cup o' kindness yet,
For auld lang syne.

Robert Burns

I am the Song

I am the song that sings the bird.
I am the leaf that grows the land.
I am the tide that moves the moon.
I am the stream that halts the sand.
I am the cloud that drives the storm.
I am the earth that lights the sun.
I am the fire that strikes the stone.
I am the clay that shapes the hand.
I am the word that speaks the man.

Charles Causley

Lord of the Dance

I danced in the morning
When the world was begun,
And I danced in the moon
And the stars and the sun
And I came down from heaven
And I danced on the earth –
At Bethlehem I had my birth.

Dance then wherever you may be;
I am the Lord of the Dance, said he,
I'll lead you all, wherever you may be,
I will lead you all in the Dance, said he.

I danced for the scribe
And the pharisee,
But they would not dance
And they couldn't follow me;
I danced for the fishermen,
For James and John –
They came with me
And the dance went on.

I danced on the Sabbath
And I cured the lame;
The holy people
Said it was a shame;
They whipped and they stripped
And they hung me high,
And they left me there
On a Cross to die.

I danced on a Friday
When the sky turned black –
It's hard to dance
With the devil on your back;
They buried my body
And they thought I'd gone –
But I am the dance
And I still go on.

They cut me down
And I leapt up high –
I am the life
That'll never, never die;
I'll live in you
If you'll live in me –
I am the Lord
Of the Dance, said he.

Dance then wherever you may be;
I am the Lord of the Dance, said he,
I'll lead you all, wherever you may be,
I will lead you all in the Dance, said he.

Sydney Carter

Skye Boat Song

Sing me a song of a lad that is gone,
Say, could that lad be I?
Merry of soul he sailed on a day
Over the sea to Skye.

Mull was astern, Rum on the port,
Eigg on the starboard bow;
Glory of youth glowed in his soul:
Where is that glory now?

Sing me a song of a lad that is gone,
Say, could that lad be I?
Merry of soul he sailed on a day
Over the sea to Skye.

Give me again all that was there,
Give me the sun that shone!
Give me the eyes, give me the soul,
Give me the lad that's gone!

Sing me a song of a lad that is gone,
Say, could that lad be I?
Merry of soul he sailed on a day
Over the sea to Skye.

Billow and breeze, islands and seas,
Mountains of rain and sun,
All that was good, all that was fair,
All that was me is gone.

Robert Louis Stevenson

Pinda Cake

De pinda cake lady comin' down
With her basket an' glass case she comin' to town,
She stop by de school gate an' set up her stall,
An' while she a-set up, hear de ole lady bawl;

Pinda! Pinda cake!
Pinda! Pinda cake!
Gal an' bwoy me jus' done bake,
Come buy yuh lovely pinda cake!

She have grater cake an' she have duckunoo,
Coconut drops an' bulla cake too,
Jackass corn an' plantain tart,
But the t'ing dat dearest to me heart

Is Pinda! Pinda cake!
Pinda! Pinda cake!
Gal an' bwoy me jus' done bake,
Come buy yuh lovely pinda cake!

We all crowd round her an' yuh can tell
By de look o' de cake dem, an' de spicy smell
Dat they won't stay in de glass case fe too long,
As we buy from de lady, we join in de song.

Pinda! Pinda cake!
Pinda! Pinda cake!
Gal an' bwoy me jus' done bake,
Come buy yuh lovely pinda cake!

Valerie Bloom

Python on Piccolo

Python on piccolo
Dingo on drums,
Gannet on gee-tar
Sits and strums.

Croc on cornet
Goes to town,
Sloth on sitar
Upside-down.

Toad on tuba
Sweet and strong,
Crane on clarinet,
Goat on gong.
And the sun jumped up in the morning.

Toucan travelling
On trombone,
Zebra zapping
On xylophone.

Beaver on bugle
Late and soon,
Boa constrictor
On bassoon.

Tiger on trumpet
Blows a storm,
Flying fox
On flügelhorn.
And the sun jumped up in the morning.

Frog on fiddle,
Hippo on harp,
Owl on oboe
Flat and sharp.

Viper on vibes
Soft and low,
Pelican
On pi-a-no.

Dromedary
On double-bass
Cheetah on 'cello
Giving chase.
And the sun jumped up in the morning.

Charles Causley

Daisy

Daisy, Daisy,
Give me your answer do,
I'm half crazy
All for the love of you;
It won't be a stylish marriage,
For I can't afford a carriage –
But you'll look sweet
Upon the seat
Of a bicycle made for two!

Anon.

The Song of the Jellicles

Jellicle Cats come out to-night
Jellicle Cats come one come all:
The Jellicle Moon is shining bright –
Jellicles come to the Jellicle Ball.

Jellicle Cats are black and white,
Jellicle Cats are rather small;
Jellicle Cats are merry and bright,
And pleasant to hear when they caterwaul.
Jellicle Cats have cheerful faces,
Jellicle Cats have bright black eyes;
They like to practise their airs and graces
And wait for the Jellicle Moon to rise.

Jellicle Cats develop slowly,
Jellicle Cats are not too big;
Jellicle Cats are roly-poly,
They know how to dance a gavotte and a jig.
Until the Jellicle Moon appears
They make their toilette and take their repose:
Jellicles wash behind their ears,
Jellicles dry between their toes.

Jellicle Cats are white and black,
Jellicle Cats are of moderate size;
Jellicles jump like a jumping-jack;
Jellicle Cats have moonlit eyes.
They're quiet enough in the morning hours,
They're quiet enough in the afternoon,
Reserving their terpsichorean powers
To dance by the light of the Jellicle Moon.

Jellicle Cats are black and white,
Jellicle Cats (as I said) are small;
If it happens to be a stormy night
They will practise a caper or two in the hall.
If it happens the sun is shining bright
You would say they had nothing to do at all:
They are resting and saving themselves to be right
For the Jellicle moon and the Jellicle Ball.

T. S. Eliot

from *The Song of Hiawatha*

Blessing the Cornfields

Sing, O Song of Hiawatha,
Of the happy days that followed,
In the land of the Ojibways,
In the pleasant land and peaceful!
Sing the mysteries of Mondamin,
Sing the Blessing of the Cornfields!
Buried was the bloody hatchet,
Buried was the dreadful war-club,
Buried were all warlike weapons,
And the war-cry was forgotten.
There was peace among the nations;
Unmolested roved the hunters,
Built the birch canoe for sailing,
Caught the fish in lake and river,
Shot the deer and trapped the beaver;
Unmolested worked the women,
Made their sugar from the maple,
Gathered wild rice in the meadows,
Dressed the skins of deer and beaver.
All around the happy village
Stood the maize-fields, green and shining,
Waved the green plumes of Mondamin,
Waved his soft and sunny tresses,
Filling all the land with plenty.
'Twas the women who in spring-time
Planted the broad fields and fruitful,

Buried in the earth Mondamin;
'Twas the women who in autumn
Stripped the yellow husks of harvest,
Stripped the garments from Mondamin,
Even as Hiawatha taught them.

H. W. Longfellow

Performance
Poems

Poems that are specifically written to be performed out
loud by a single voice or a group. They may not look like
poems written down, but it's not what they look like that's
important, it's what they sound like!

Fruit Picking

Raspberry, strawberry, gooseberry, plum,
Fruit picking time is really good fun;
Out in the field, in our hats, in the sun,
Raspberry, strawberry, gooseberry, plum.

Gooseberry, strawberry, raspberry, plum,
Carefully picking with finger and thumb;
When the baskets are full our picking is done,
Gooseberry, strawberry, raspberry, plum.

Raspberry, gooseberry, strawberry, plum,
Here is a tune for pickers to hum;
Tap out the beat like the sound of a drum,
Raspberry, gooseberry, strawberry, plum.

Raspberry, strawberry, gooseberry, plum,
Now in our beds when night-time has come
We can think of our wonderful day in the sun,
Raspberry, strawberry, gooseberry, plum.

Jack Ousbey

The Dragon Who Ate Our School

– 1 –

The day the dragon came to call,
she ate the gate, the playground wall
and, slate by slate, the roof and all,
the staffroom, gym, and entrance hall,
and every classroom, big or small.

So . . .
She's undeniably great.
She's absolutely cool,
the dragon who ate
the dragon who ate
the dragon who ate our school.

– 2 –

Pupils panicked. Teachers ran.
She flew at them with wide wingspan.
She slew a few and then began
to chew through the lollipop man,
two parked cars and a transit van.

Wow . . .!
She's undeniably great.
She's absolutely cool,
the dragon who ate
the dragon who ate
the dragon who ate our school.

– 3 –

She bit off the head of the head.
She said she was sad he was dead.
He bled and he bled and he bled.
And as she fed, her chin went red
and then she swallowed the cycle shed.

Oh . . .
She's undeniably great.
She's absolutely cool,
the dragon who ate
the dragon who ate
the dragon who ate our school.

– 4 –

It's thanks to her that we've been freed.
We needn't write. We needn't read.
Me and my mates are all agreed,
we're very pleased with her indeed.
So clear the way, let her proceed.

Cos . . .
She's undeniably great.
She's absolutely cool,
the dragon who ate
the dragon who ate
the dragon who ate our school.

– 5 –

There was some stuff she couldn't eat.
A monster forced to face defeat,
she spat it out along the street –
the dinner ladies' veg and meat
and that pink muck they serve for sweet.

But . . .
She's undeniably great.
She's absolutely cool,
the dragon who ate
the dragon who ate
the dragon who ate our school.

Nick Toczek

What Teachers Wear in Bed!

It's anybody's guess
what teachers wear in bed at night
so we held a competition
to see if any of us were right.

We did a spot of research,
although some of them wouldn't say,
but it's probably something funny
as they look pretty strange by day.

Our Headteacher's quite old-fashioned,
he wears a Victorian nightshirt,
our sports teacher wears her tracksuit
and sometimes her netball skirt.

That new teacher in the infants
wears bedsocks with see-through pyjamas,
our Deputy Head wears a T-shirt
he brought back from the Bahamas.

We asked our secretary what she wore
but she shooed us out of her room
and our teacher said, her favourite nightie
and a splash of expensive perfume.

And Mademoiselle, who teaches French,
is really very rude
she whispered, '*Alors!* Don't tell a soul,
but I sleep in the . . . back bedroom!'

Brian Moses

There's a Monster in the Garden

If the water in your fishpond fizzes and foams
And there's giant teeth marks on the plastic gnomes
You've found huge claw prints in the flower bed
And just caught side of a two-horned head
Put a stick in your front lawn with a piece of card on
Look out everybody – there's a monster in the garden!

You haven't seen the dustman for several weeks
Haven't seen the gasman who was looking for leaks
Haven't seen the paper-girl, postman or plumber
Haven't seen the window cleaner since last summer
Don't mean to be nosy, I do beg your pardon
Look out everybody – there's a monster in the garden!

One dark night it will move in downstairs
Start living in the kitchen, take you unawares
Frighten you, bite on you, with howls and roars
It will crash about, smash about, push you out of doors
In the cold and snow the ice and rain will harden
Look out everybody – there's a monster in the garden!

Now listen to me, neighbour, all of this is true
It happened next door, now it's happening to you.
There's something nasty on the compost heap
Spends all day there curled up asleep
You don't want your bones crunched or jarred on
Look out everybody – there's a monster in the garden!

David Harmer

Leisure Centre, Pleasure Centre

You go through plate glass doors
with giant red handles,
into light that's as bright
as a million candles.
The chlorine smells
the whole place steaming,
the kids are yelling
and the kids are screaming.

Watch them
    wave jump
    dive thump
    cartwheel
    free wheel
    look cute
    slip chute
    toe stub
    nose rub
    in the leisure centre, pleasure centre.

Sporty people laugh and giggle
folk in swimsuits give a wiggle.
Kids are in the café busy thinking
if they can afford some fizzy drinking.
In the changing rooms
wet folk shiver.
It's hard to get dressed
when you shake and quiver.

And we go
    breast stroke
    back stroke
    two stroke
    big folk
    hair soak
    little folk
    eye poke
    no joke
    in the leisure centre, pleasure centre.

And now we're driving back home
fish 'n' chips in the car,
eyes are slowly closing
but it's not very far.
Snuggle wuggle up in fresh clean sheets
a leisure centre trip
is the best of treats because you can
   keep fit
   leap sit
   eat crisps
   do twists
   belly flop
   pit stop
   fill up
   with 7-Up
   get going
   blood flowing
   look snappy
   be happy
in the leisure centre, pleasure centre.

John Rice

Louder!

OK, Andrew, nice and clearly – off you go.

Welcome everybody to our school concert . . .

Louder, please, Andrew. Mums and dads won't hear you at the back, will they?

Welcome everybody to our school concert . . .

Louder, Andrew. You're not trying.
Pro – ject – your – voice.
Take a b i g b r e a t h and louder!

Welcome everybody to our school concert . . .

For goodness sake, Andrew. LOUDER! LOUDER!

Welcome every body to our school concert!

Now, Andrew, there's no need to be silly.

Roger Stevens

'Genius'

I am a liric maniac
An Urban Oral GENIUS
My style iz fast 'n' FURIOUS
My manna iz SPONTANEOUS
My lirix make yer laugh sometimes
As well as bein' SERIOUS
I'll send yer round 'n' round the bend
I'll make yer act DELIRIOUS
Each word is hot, and can't be held
I suppose you'd say I'm DANGEROUS
I know I have a way with wurdz
The wurd I'd use iz NOTORIOUS
For those who want to challenge me
I find it quite RIDICULOUS
When critics try and put me down
Can't see them. They're ANONYMOUS
The only thing I have ter say
I see them all as ODIOUS
I luv my rithmz 'n' the beatz
Smell my wurdz, they're ODOROUS
I love my lirix to the max
Evry syllable 'n' sound iz MARVELLOUS
I execute my wurdz so well
I suppose you'd call it MURDEROUS
To work so hard on all these wurdz
Some say it is LABORIOUS
There's double meaning in my style
Four syllables ter you. AM . . . BIG . . . U . . . OUS

I know I'm going on and on
But I certainly ain't MONOTONOUS
You have ter chill 'n' agree with me
The feeling is UNANIMOUS
Ter get inside yer head like this
I know that I am DEVIOUS
I do it in a sneaky way
I suppose I'd say MISCHIEVOUS
When pepul think about my rimez,
I know that they are CURIOUS
Don't understand the resun why
Becuze the cluez R OBVIOUS
Okay you're right, my wurdz 'R' good
I suppose they are MIRACULOUS
Astounded by this type of rime
I know you 'R' OBLIVIOUS
There'z only one thing left ter say
I'm bad 'n' cool
'N' INFAMOUS.

Martin Glynn

Pencil Me In

I know a pencil
Full of lead,
It knows the thoughts
Within my head,
It knows my secrets
And my fears,
It draws a line
Right through my tears.
I know a pencil
Old and grey,
Willing to work
Both night and day,
Fat and lovely
Light and fine,
It moves with me
Through space and time.

Be they good
Or be they bad,
It tells of all
The dreams I have,
And when I have
No oar to row,
It writes a way
And lets me go.
When baby words
Are crying loud,
It touches words
And makes me proud,
A work of art
It is no fake,
It really has
A point to make.

This pencil sees
The best of me,
The worst
And all the rest
Of me,
And as I go
Through puberty,
It changes all my
Poetry.
It goes with me
On all my tours,
It fought with me
In all word wars,
And peacefully
This pencil tries
To help me learn
And make me wise.

Every pencil needs a hand
And every mind needs to expand,
I know a pencil,
What you see
Is me and it
In harmony.

Benjamin Zephaniah

Word of a Lie

I am the fastest runner in my school and that's
NO WORD OF A LIE
I've got gold fillings in my teeth and that's
NO WORD OF A LIE
In my garden, I've got my own big bull and that's
NO WORD OF A LIE
I'm brilliant at giving my enemies grief and that's
NO WORD OF A LIE
I can multiply three billion and twenty-seven by nine billion
  four thousand and one in two seconds and that's
NO WORD OF A LIE
I can calculate the distance between planets before you've
  had toast and that's
NO WORD OF A LIE
I can always tell when my best pals boast and that's
NO WORD OF A LIE
I'd been round the world twice before I was three and a
  quarter and that's
NO WORD OF A LIE
I am definitely my mother's favourite daughter and that's
NO WORD OF A LIE
I am brilliant at fake laughter. I go Ha aha Ha ha ha and
  that's
NO WORD OF A LIE
I can tell the weather from one look at the sky and that's
NO WORD OF A LIE
I can predict disasters, floods, earthquakes and murders and
  that's

NO WORD OF A LIE
I can always tell when other people lie and that's
NO WORD OF A LIE
I can even tell if someone is going to die and that's
NO WORD OF A LIE
I am the most popular girl in my entire school and that's
NO WORD OF A LIE
I know the golden rule, don't play the fool, don't boast, be
  shy and that's
NO WORD OF A LIE
I am sensitive, I listen, I have kind brown eyes and that's
NO WORD OF A LIE

You don't believe me do you?
ALL RIGHT, ALL RIGHT, ALL RIGHT
I am the biggest liar in my school and that's
NO WORD OF A LIE

Jackie Kay

The Sound Collector

A stranger called this morning
Dressed all in black and grey
Put every sound into a bag
And carried them away

The whistling of the kettle
The turning of the lock
The purring of the kitten
The ticking of the clock

The popping of the toaster
The crunching of the flakes
When you spread the marmalade
The scraping noise it makes

The hissing of the frying-pan
The ticking of the grill
The bubbling of the bathtub
As it starts to fill

The drumming of the raindrops
On the window-pane
When you do the washing-up
The gurgle of the drain

The crying of the baby
The squeaking of the chair
The swishing of the curtain
The creaking of the stair

A stranger called this morning
He didn't leave his name
Left us only silence
Life will never be the same.

Roger McGough

Raps

A type of performance poetry based on strong rhythm, rapid pace and repetition. Used in modern music and is associated with Caribbean and Afro-Caribbean cultures.

Wurd Up

Blowin like a hurricane
Destroyin all the competishan
Kickin up the lirix hard
There ain't no opposishan
Coz
Wen I'm on a roll like this
I'm jus like a physishan
Like a boxer . . . punch you out
With lirical precishan
Flowin like a river
Jus
Flying like a bird
'N'
Checkin out the ridim
Just takin in my wurdz
I'tz time
Ter climb
'n' rime
The sign
Jus growz
'n' flowz
'n' showz
'n' throwz
a skill
Ter thrill
'n' kill
Jus chill
Coz

I'm
Stingin like a nettle
Jus bitin like a flea
Smoother than a baby's skin
Much ruffer than the sea
Colder than an icicle
Hotta than the sun
Lirix always on the move
Like bullets from a gun
Much noizier than thunder
Much cooler than the rain
I'm fitta than an exercise
Deep within the brain
Sharpa than a needle
More solid than a rock
Repeatin like an echo
As rhythmic as a clock
More dangerus than a lion
Much louda than a plane
As quiet as a whisper
I burn yer like a flame
Fasta than a jaguar
Slowa than a snail
Yeah! rapid like a heartbeat
Tuffa than a nail
More painful than a scratch
As tasty as food
Horrible like a medicine
My lirix change yer mood
As tasty as a mango

422

As bitter as a lime
Softa than a coconut
Endless as the time
Kickin like a reggae song
Much sadda than the blues
I'm as tiring as a marathon
Give yer all the newz
Wilda than a stampede
As gentle as a breeze
Irritatin as a cough
More wicked than a sneeze
More lively than a child
Romantic that's me
Still harsh like the winter
Jus buzzin like a bee
The rimes 'n' times are signs
to blow 'n' show a flow

The wurdz

WURD UP!

Martin Glynn

Patchwork Rap

I'm a touch lazy
Don't like doing much work
But often get the itch
To pitch into some patchwork
It may be a hotchpotch
Like fretwork or such work
When I slouch on my couch
And I fetch out my patchwork

First I snatch a patch
From the batch in my pouch
But the patch doesn't match
The patches on my patchwork
So I catch another patch
From the batch in my satchel
And this one matches
The patches on my patchwork.
So I take my patch
And attach it with stitches
Patch against patch
Where the patchwork matches
But if it doesn't match
Even after it's attached
Then the mismatched stitch
Has to be detached.

I don't like thatchwork
Don't like ditchwork
Only kind I favour
Is my patchwork stitchwork
And soon my patchwork's
Going like clockwork
Sharper than a pitchfork
Neater than brickwork
Hotter than a firework
Cooler than a waxwork.

So I snatch a patch
From the batch in my pouch
But the patch doesn't match
The patches on my patchwork
So I catch another patch
From the batch in my satchel
And this one matches
The patches on my patchwork.

So I take my patch
And attach it with stitches
Patch it against patch
Where the patchwork matches
And I keep on patching
Till everything's matching
And I keep on stitching
Till I've filled up the kitchen
with my rich rich rich rich
Wider than a soccer pitch
Wonderful colourful patchwork quilt!

Now which stitch is which?

Adrian Mitchell

Baby-K Rap Rhyme

My name is Baby-K
An dis is my rhyme
Sit back folks
While I rap my mind;

Ah rocking with my homegirl,
My Mommy
Ah rocking with my homeboy,
My Daddy
My big sister, Les, an
My Granny,
Hey dere people – my posse
I'm the business
The ruler of the nursery

poop po-doop
poop-poop po-doop
poop po-doop
poop-poop po-doop

Well, ah soaking up de rhythm
Ah drinking up my tea
Ah bouncing an ah rocking
On my Mommy knee
So happy man so happy

poop po-doop
poop-poop po-doop
poop po-doop
poop-poop po-doop

Wish my rhyme wasn't hard
Wish my rhyme wasn't rough
But sometimes, people
You got to be tough

Cause dey pumping up de chickens
Dey stumping down de trees
Dey messing up de ozones
Dey messing up de seas
Baby-K say, stop dis –
please, please, please

poop po-doop
poop-poop po-doop
poop po-doop
poop-poop po-doop

Now am splashing in de bath
With my rubber duck
Who don't like dis rhyme
Kiss my baby-foot
Babies everywhere
Join a Babyhood

Cause dey hotting up de globe, man
Dey hitting down de seals
Dey killing off de ellies
for dere ivories
Baby-K say, stop dis –
please, please, please

poop po-doop
poop-poop po-doop
poop po-doop
poop-poop po-doop

Dis is my Baby-K rap
But it's kinda plea
What kinda world
Dey going to leave fuh me?
What kinda world
Dey going to leave fuh me?

Poop po-doop.

Grace Nichols

Write-A-Rap Rap

Hey, everybody, let's write a rap.
First there's a rhythm you'll need to clap.
Keep that rhythm and stay in time,
'cause a rap needs rhythm and a good strong rhyme.

The rhyme keeps coming in the very same place
so don't fall behind and try not to race.
The rhythm keeps the tap on a regular beat
and the rhyme helps to wrap your rap up neat.

'But what'll we write?' I hear you shout.
There ain't no rules for what a rap's about.
You can rap about a robber, you can rap about a king,
you can rap about a chewed up piece of string . . .
(well, you can rap about almost . . . anything!)

You can rap about the ceiling, you can rap about the floor,
you can rap about the window, write a rap on the door.
You can rap about things that are mean or pleasant,
you can rap about wrapping up a Christmas present.

You can rap about a mystery hidden in a box,
you can rap about a pair of smelly old socks.
You can rap about something that's over and gone,
you can rap about something going on and on and on and
on . . .

But when you think there just ain't nothing left to say . . .
you can wrap it all up and put it away.
It's a rap. It's a rap. It's a rap rap rap rap RAP!

Tony Mitton

Everybody Rap

Can you do a rap?
        Can you do a rap?
Can you make a rhyme?
        Can you make a rhyme?
Can you link up words,
        Can you link up words,
To help me blow my mind?
        To help me blow my mind?

    Poetry's the thing
    that we can do
    To show there's no difference
    Between me and you.

Black and white
are all the same
And those who say different
are mad insane.

Do you agree?
I said do you agree?
If you agree,
Say yowl to me.

SuAndi

Gran, Can You Rap?

Gran was in her chair she was taking a nap
When I tapped her on the shoulder to see if she could rap.
Gran, can you rap? Can you rap? Can you, Gran?
And she opened one eye and she said to me, Man,
　　I'm the best rapping Gran this world's ever seen
　　I'm a tip-top, slip-slap, rap-rap queen.

And she rose from her chair in the corner of the room
And she started to rap with a bim-bam-boom,
And she rolled up her eyes and she rolled round her head
And as she rolled by this is what she said,
　　I'm the best rapping Gran this world's ever seen
　　I'm a nip-nap, yip-yap, rap-rap queen.

Then she rapped past my dad and she rapped past my
    mother,
She rapped past me and my little baby brother.
She rapped her arms narrow she rapped her arms wide,
She rapped through the door and she rapped outside.
    She's the best rapping Gran this world's ever seen
    She's a drip-drop, trip-trap, rap-rap queen.

She rapped down the garden she rapped down the street,
The neighbours all cheered and they tapped their feet.
She rapped through the traffic lights as they turned red
As she rapped round the corner this is what she said,
    I'm the best rapping Gran this world's ever seen
    I'm a flip-flop, hip-hop, rap-rap queen.

She rapped down the lane she rapped up the hill,
And as she disappeared she was rapping still.
I could hear Gran's voice saying, Listen, Man,
Listen to the rapping of the rap-rap Gran.
    I'm the best rapping Gran this world's ever seen
    I'm a –
        tip-top, slip-slap,
          nip-nap, yip-yap,
            hip-hop, trip-trap,
              touch yer cap,
              take a nap,
                happy, happy, happy, happy,
                rap—— rap—— queen.

Jack Ousbey

Haircut Rap

Ah sey, ah want it short,
Short back an' side,
Ah tell him man, ah tell him
When ah teck him aside,
Ah sey, ah want a haircut
Ah can wear with pride,
So lef' it long on top
But short back an' side.

Ah sey try an put a pattern
In the shorter part,
Yuh could put a skull an' crossbone,
Or an arrow through a heart,
Meck sure ah have enough hair lef'
Fe cover me wart,
Lef a likkle pon the top,
But the res' – keep it short.

Well, bwoy, him start to cut
An' me settle down to wait,
Him was cuttin' from seven
Till half-past eight,
Ah was startin' to get worried
'cause ah see it gettin' late,
But then him put the scissors down
Sey 'There yuh are, mate.'

Well ah did see a skull an a
Criss-cross bone or two,
But was me own skull an bone
That was peepin' through,
Ah look jus' like a monkey
Ah did see once at the zoo,
Him sey, 'What's de matter, Tammy,
Don't yuh like the hair-do?'

Well, ah feel me heart stop beatin'
When me look pon me reflection,
Ah feel like somet'ing frizzle up
Right in me middle section
Ah look aroun' fe somewhey
Ah could crawl into an' hide
The day ah mek me brother cut
Me hair short back an' side.

Valerie Bloom

Cool Cat

Well I'm a cat with nine
And I'm in my prime
I'm a Casanova Cat
And I'm feline fine
I'm strolling down the street
In my white slipper feet
Yeh, all the little lady cats
Are looking for a treat
Because I got style
I got a naughty smile
I'm gonna cross this street
In just a little while
    to be with you
    to be with you
    to be with you
    to be with
You got grace
You got a lickable face
I'm gonna love ya and leave ya
And you'll never find a trace
Because I'm on my own
I like to be alone
I'm just a swingin', strollin',
Rollin' stone
But it's your lucky day
I'm gonna pass your way
I can spare a little lovin'
If you wanna stop and

play with me
play with me
play with me
play with
Meeow my
I got a twinkling eye
I'm gonna cross this street
So don't you be too shy
But what's this I see
Comin' straight at me
It's a crazy car driver
Tryin' to make me flee
So I look up slow
Just to let the man know
That I don't go any faster
Than I really wanna . . .

X ! X ! X ! X ! X ! X

Well I'm a cat with eight
I guess he couldn't wait
But I'm looking good
And I'm feline great!

Mike Jubb

Choral Poems

Poetry written for more than one voice specifically
to be performed.

Picnic Time on the M25

A true story! What a daft place for a picnic! P.S. the M69 is much nicer. By the way it's fun to repeat each line when performing the verses.

Picnic time go for a ride
set your sights on the countryside
pack the car and start to drive
stop by the side stop by the side
stop by the side of the M25

Deckchairs on the grass verge
Watch the traffic pass NEEOWN!
Try and pour your flask
Ooh ah ooh ooh eeh
Boiling coffee on your knee

Picnic time go for a ride
set your sights on the countryside
pack the car and start to drive
stop by the side stop by the side
stop by the side of the M25

Salmon spread wholemeal bread
Try to eat as you move your head
Left to right try to bite
Oooh ah ooh ooh eeh
Salmon spread on your knee

Picnic time go for a ride
set your sights on the countryside
pack the car and start to drive
stop by the side stop by the side
stop by the side of the M25

Picnic time on the M25
Toxic gases will collide
Car-bon di-oxide
Breathe in SNIFF!
Breathe in SNIFF!
Petrol fumes and lead oxide
Cough splutter cough choke
Poisoned lungs are no joke
Ooh ah ooh ooh eeh
Plan your picnics carefully
Seaside or countryside
But don't go down to the M25
Don't go down to the M25
Don't – pic – nic – on – the – M – Twenty-Five!

Paul Cookson

All of Us Knocking on the Stable Door

Three great kings, three wise men
Tramp across the desert to Bethlehem
Arrive at the inn, don't travel no more
they start knocking at the stable door.

Knocking at the door, knocking at the door
All of us are knocking at the stable door.

I've got myrrh, he's got gold
He's got frankincense and all of us are cold
We stand here shivering, chilled to the core
We're just knocking on the stable door.

The star above it glows in the sky
Burning up the darkness and we know why
A baby king's asleep in the straw
So we start knocking on the stable door.

Travelled some distance, we've travelled far
Melchior, Casper and Balthazaar
We are so wealthy, the baby's so poor
But here we are knocking on the stable door.

Now is the time, now is the hour
To feel the glory, worship the power
We quietly enter, kneel on the floor
Just the other side of the stable door.

Knocking on the door, knocking on the door
All of us knocking at the stable door.

Knocking on the door, knocking on the door
We're all knocking on the stable door.

David Harmer

Barefoot

This poem was written in Jamaica, and is to be spoken out loud. One person says the line of action, whilst the rest of the group/class chant the chorus INNA YUH BAREFOOT.

Yuh can jump
    Inna yuh barefoot!
Yuh can run
    Inna yuh barefoot!
Yuh can walk strong
    Inna yuh barefoot!
Yuh can walk near
    Inna yuh barefoot!
Yuh can walk far
    Inna yuh barefoot!
Yuh can guh a markit
    Inna yuh barefoot!
Yuh can guh a riva
    Inna yuh barefoot!

Yuh can guh a sea
    Inna yuh barefoot!
Yuh can pray
    Inna yuh barefoot!
Yuh can dance
    Inna yuh barefoot!
Yuh can rap
    Inna yuh barefoot!
Yuh can guh a skool
    Inna yuh barefoot!
Yuh feel free
    Inna yuh barefoot!
Yuh feel good
    Inna yuh barefoot!
Yuh feel ire
    Inna yuh barefoot!
You can climb coconut tree
    Inna yuh barefoot!
Yuh can kick a football
    Inna yuh barefoot!
De sun nice
    Inna yuh barefoot!
De rain sweet
    Inna yuh barefoot!
Yuh skin tuff
    Inna yuh barefoot!
Yuh toes ruff
    Inna yuh barefoot!
But!
If yuh mash up yuh toes

Inna yuh barefoot!
Get a cut
Inna yuh barefoot!
Bruk yuh toes
Inna yuh barefoot!
Yuh cyaan walk
Inna yuh barefoot!
So step cool
Inna yuh barefoot!
Doan ac' fool
Inna yuh barefoot!
Ah yuh will always walk
Inna yuh barefoot!
Jus cool
Inna yuh barefoot!
Jus nice
Inna yuh barefoot!
Yuh can do anyting
Inna yuh barefoot!!!!!

Martin Glynn

Mister Moore

Mister Moore, Mister Moore
Creaking down the corridor.

Uh uh eh eh uh
Uh uh eh eh uh

Mister Moore wears wooden suits
Mister Moore's got great big boots
Mister Moore's got hair like a brush
And Mister Moore don't like me much.

Mister Moore, Mister Moore
Creaking down the corridor.

Uh uh eh eh uh
Uh uh eh eh uh

When my teacher's there I haven't got a care
I can do my sums, I can do gerzinters
When Mister Moore comes through the door
Got a wooden head filled with splinters.

Mister Moore, Mister Moore
Creaking down the corridor.

Uh uh eh eh uh
Uh uh eh eh uh

Mister Moore I implore
My earholes ache, my head is sore
Don't come through that classroom door.
Don't come through that classroom door.

Uh uh eh eh uh
Uh uh eh eh uh

Big voice, big hands
Big voice he's a very big man
Take my advice, be good be very very nice
Be good be very very nice
To Mister Moore, Mister Moore
Creaking down the corridor.

Uh uh eh eh uh
Uh uh eh eh uh

Mister Moore wears wooden suits
Mister Moore's got great big boots
Mister Moore's got hair like a brush
And Mister Moore don't like me much.

Mister Moore, Mister Moore
Creaking down the corridor.

Uh uh eh eh uh
Uh uh eh eh uh

David Harmer

I Wrote Me a Poem

I wrote me a poem, and the poem pleased me.
I told my poem to the big oak tree.
My poem went: 'Fiddle-eye-dee'.

I wrote me a sonnet, and the sonnet pleased me.
I told my sonnet to the big oak tree.
My sonnet went: 'ooh, love!' (*action: do a loud kiss*)
My poem went: 'Fiddle-eye-dee'.

I wrote me an ode, and the ode pleased me.
I told my ode to the big oak tree.
My ode went: 'lah . . . dah'.
My sonnet went: 'ooh, love!' (loud kiss)
My poem went: 'Fiddle-eye-dee'.

I wrote me an epic, and the epic pleased me.
I told my epic to the big oak tree.
My epic went: 'Too long, much too long'. (*stretch out arms*)
My ode went: 'lah . . . dah'.
My sonnet went: 'ooh, love!' (loud kiss)
My poem went: 'Fiddle-eye-dee'.

I wrote me a verse, and the verse pleased me.
I told my verse to the big oak tree.
My verse went: 'Tickety-boo, tickety-boo'.
My epic went: 'Too long, much too long'. (stretch out arms)
My ode went: 'lah . . . dah'.
My sonnet went: 'ooh, love!' (loud kiss)
My poem went: 'Fiddle-eye-dee'.

I wrote me a haiku, and the haiku pleased me.
I told my haiku to the big oak tree.
My haiku went: 'Slooooow thought'.
My verse went: 'Tickety-boo, tickety-boo'.
My epic went: 'Too long, much too long'. (stretch out arms)
My ode went: 'lah . . . dah'.
My sonnet went: 'ooh, love!' (loud kiss)
My poem went: 'Fiddle-eye-dee'.

I wrote me a rhyme, and the rhyme pleased me.
I told my rhyme to the big oak tree.
My rhyme went: 'Sky high'. (stretch arms upwards)
My haiku went: 'Slooooow thought'.
My verse went: 'Tickety-boo, tickety-boo'.
My epic went: 'Too long, much too long'. (stretch out arms)
My ode went: 'lah . . . dah'.
My sonnet went: 'ooh, love!' (loud kiss)
My poem went: 'Fiddle-eye-dee'.

I wrote me a limerick, and the limerick pleased me.
I told my limerick to the big oak tree.
My limerick went: 'Silly-billy'. (*wag finger*)
My rhyme went: 'Sky high'. (*stretch arms upwards*)
My haiku went: 'Slooooow thought'.
My verse went: 'Tickety-boo, tickety-boo'.
My epic went: 'Too long, much too long'. (*stretch out arms*)
My ode went: 'lah . . . dah'.
My sonnet went: 'ooh, love!' (*loud kiss*)
My poem went: 'Fiddle-eye-dee'.

I wrote me a song, and the song pleased me.
I told my song to the big oak tree.
My song went: 'Tree Shanty'.
My limerick went: 'Silly-billy'. (*wag finger*)
My rhyme went: 'Sky high'. (*stretch arms upwards*)
My haiku went: 'Slooooow thought'.
My verse went: 'Tickety-boo, tickety-boo'.
My epic went: 'Too long, much too long'. (*stretch out arms*)
My ode went: 'lah . . . dah'.
My sonnet went: 'ooh, love!' (*loud kiss*)
My poem went: 'Fiddle-eye-dee'.

I wrote me some words, and the words pleased me.
I told my words to the big oak tree.
My words went: 'Jibber-jabber'.
My song went: 'Tree Shanty'.
My limerick went: 'Silly-billy'. (wag finger)
My rhyme went: 'Sky high'. (stretch arms upwards)
My haiku went: 'Slooooow thought'.
My verse went: 'Tickety-boo, tickety-boo'.
My epic went: 'Too long, much too long'. (stretch out arms)
My ode went: 'lah . . . dah'.
My sonnet went: 'ooh, love!' (loud kiss)
My poem went: 'Fiddle-eye-dee'.

Bruce Barnes

Narrative Poems

A poem which will tell a story.
Ballads are an example of narrative poems.

from *The Highwayman*

The wind was a torrent of darkness among the gusty trees,
The moon was a ghostly galleon tossed upon cloudy seas,
The road was a ribbon of moonlight over the purple moor,
And the highwayman came riding –
    Riding – riding –
The highwayman came riding, up to the old inn-door.

He'd a French cocked-hat on his forehead, a bunch of lace
    at his chin,
A coat of claret velvet, and breeches of brown doe skin;
They fitted with never a wrinkle: his boots were up to the
    thigh!
And he rode with a jewelled tinkle,
    His pistol butts a-twinkle,
His rapier hilt a-twinkle, under the jewelled sky.

Over the cobbles he clattered and clashed in the dark inn-
    yard,
And he tapped with his whip on the shutters, but all was
    locked and barred;
He whistled a tune to the window, and who should be
    waiting there
But the landlord's black-eyed daughter,
    Bess, the landlord's daughter,
Plaiting a dark red love-knot into her long black hair.

And dark in the old inn-yard a stable-wicket creaked
Where Tim the ostler listened; his face was white and
    peaked;
His eyes were hollows of madness, his hair like mouldy hay,
But he loved the landlord's daughter,
   The landlord's red-lipped daughter;
Dumb as a dog he listened, and he heard the robber say –

'One kiss, my bonny sweetheart, I'm after a prize tonight,
But I shall be back with the yellow gold before the morning
    light;
Yet, if they press me sharply, and harry me through the day,
Then look for me by moonlight,
   Watch for me by moonlight,
I'll come to thee by moonlight, though hell should bar the
    way.'

He rose upright in the stirrups; he scarce could reach her
    hand,
But she loosened her hair i' the casement! His face burnt like
    a brand
As the black cascade of perfume came tumbling over his
    breast;
And he kissed its waves in the moonlight,
   (Oh, sweet black waves in the moonlight!)
Then he tugged at his rein in the moonlight, and galloped
    away to the west.

Alfred Noyes

The Listeners

'Is there anybody there?' said the Traveller,
Knocking on the moonlit door;
And his horse in the silence champed the grasses
Of the forest's ferny floor;
And a bird flew up out of the turret,
Above the Traveller's head:
And he smote upon the door again a second time;
'Is there anybody there?' he said.
But no one descended to the Traveller;
No head from the leaf fringed sill
Leaned over and looked into his grey eyes,
Where he stood perplexed and still.
But only a host of phantom listeners
That dwelt in the lone house then
Stood listening in the quiet of the moonlight
To that voice from the world of men:
Stood thronging the faint moonbeams on the dark stair,
That goes down to the empty hall,
Hearkening in an air stirred and shaken
By the lonely Traveller's call.
And he felt in his heart their strangeness,
Their stillness answering his cry,
While his horse moved, cropping the dark turf,
'Neath the starred and leafy sky;
For he suddenly smote on the door, even
Louder, and lifted his head: –
'Tell them I came, and no one answered,
That I kept my word,' he said.

Never the least stir made the listeners,
Though every word he spake
Fell echoing through the shadowiness of the still house
From the one man left awake:
Ay, they heard his foot upon the stirrup,
And the sound of iron on stone,
And how the silence surged softly backward,
When the plunging hoofs were gone.

Walter de la Mare

Kubla Khan

In Xanadu did Kubla Khan
A stately pleasure-dome decree:
Where Alph, the sacred river, ran
Through caverns measureless to man
   Down to a sunless sea.
So twice five miles of fertile ground
With walls and towers were girdled round:
And here were gardens bright with sinuous rills,
Where blossomed many an incense-bearing tree;
And here were forests ancient as the hills
Enfolding sunny spots of greenery.
But oh! that deep romantic chasm which slanted
Down the green hill athwart and a cedarn cover!
A savage place! as holy and enchanted
As e'er beneath a waning moon was haunted

By woman wailing for her demon-lover!
And from this chasm, with ceaseless turmoil seething,
As if this earth in fast thick pants were breathing,
A mighty fountain momently was forced:
Amid whose swift half-intermitted burst
Huge fragments vaulted like a rebounding hail,
Or chaffy grain beneath the thrasher's flail;
And 'mid these dancing rocks at once and ever
It flung up momently the sacred river.
Five miles meandering with a mazy motion
Through wood and dale the sacred river ran,
Then reached the caverns measureless to man,
And sank in tumult to a lifeless ocean:
And 'mid this tumult Kubla heard from far
Ancestral voices prophesying war!
   The shadow of the dome of pleasure
   Floated midway on the waves;
   Where was heard the mingled measure
   From the fountain and the caves.
It was a miracle of rare device,
A sunny pleasure-dome with caves of ice!
   A damsel with a dulcimer
   In a vision once I saw:
   It was an Abyssinian maid,
   And on her dulcimer she played,
   Singing of Mount Abora.
   Could I revive within me
   Her symphony and song,
   To such a deep delight 'twould win me,
That with music loud and long,

I would build that dome in air,
That sunny dome! those caves of ice!
And all who heard should see them there,
And all should cry, Beware! Beware!
His flashing eyes, his floating hair!
Weave a circle round him thrice,
And close your eyes with holy dread,
For he on honey-dew hath fed,
And drunk the milk of Paradise.

S. T. Coleridge

Jack's Tale

'At day-break, Jack finding the Giant not likely to be soon
roused, crept softly out of his hiding-place, seized the hen,
and ran off with her.'
Iona and Peter Opie: The Classic Fairy Tales.

Sun rises before me,
dazzles pathless flight.
In the corner of each eye
mists drift and fade,
dissolve against a lightening sky;
the tops of oaks sprawl
like giant undergrowth below.
I dare not pause to gaze,
I dare not fall!

Behind, as if in smoke,
the castle disappears.
My life is ruled by noise:
heart drums inside my chest,
the giant thud of angry steps
invades my ears.

Beneath one arm
a squirming weight of feathers,
crooked between waist and elbow,
squawks our whereabouts into the dawn,
scratches tales of panic into flesh.
All thoughts are on escape;
all golden dreams have flown!

Ahead, at last,
green stalks emerge from cloud
then cobweb downwards,
stitching earth to sky.
I leap, grasp branches urgently
with outstretched hand;
half-slide, half-fall
to blessed earth below,
to blessed land.

Judith Nicholls

Willow Pattern

Look. On my plate
is a blue garden
It happened in China
a long time ago.

There on a bridge
the soldiers are running
to capture the princess,
the Emperor's daughter.

She left with the young man
she wanted to marry.
They fled to an island
that lay on a lake.

The Emperor was angry.
He ordered his soldiers
to capture the princess
and kill the young man.

But the man and the princess
were turned into bluebirds.
They flew from the island
and never returned.

The Emperor, in sadness,
turned into a willow.
And always he droops
as he weeps in his sorrow.

He weeps on my plate
in a blue garden.
It happened in China
a long time ago.

Tony Mitton

Maggie and the Dinosaur

Maggie ran madly round the museum –
And what do you think she saw?
A mighty tiger whose grin grew wider,
Fishes and fossils galore:
And stretching up to the ceiling
Was a rattling dinosaur.

'I'm only made of wire and bones,'
The dinosaur seemed to say;
'Everyone stands and looks at me,
But nobody wants to play.'

Maggie just froze in amazement,
Watching the dinosaur's jaw:
He spoke in a dusty whisper,
Not an earth-shattering roar.

She tried to pretend this was normal
As they passed the time of day,
Waiting until the attendant
Was looking the other way.

The dinosaur groaned as he shifted his bones
All the way to the lift,
But when the door slid open
Maggie knew he just wouldn't fit.

And so they made a break for it,
But Maggie took great care
That nobody would notice them
As they shuffled towards the stairs.

Every time they met someone
The dinosaur stopped on the spot,
And people said, 'Look – another one!
We thought we'd seen the lot!!'

They slithered slowly inch by inch
Across the entrance hall,
Then the dinosaur doubled his neck up
To squeeze through the double front door.

He clattered down the steps outside,
Running into the sun
Towards a brightly painted van
That attracted everyone.

When Maggie managed to reach him,
The dinosaur was near to tears:
'This is what I've waited for
For two hundred million years!'

A look of unspeakable happiness
Spread across his face –
But as people stared at the dinosaur,
He just gazed into space.

'I've tasted nothing like it,
It's a marvellous magical dream,
It's all I ever wanted –
A freshly whipped strawberry ice cream!'

Dave Ward

The Charge of the Light Brigade

Half a league, half a league,
Half a league onward,
All in the valley of Death
   Rode the six hundred.
    'Forward, the Light Brigade!
Charge for the guns!' he said.
Into the valley of Death
   Rode the six hundred.

'Forward, the Light Brigade!'
Was there a man dismayed?
Not though the soldier knew
   Some one had blundered.
Theirs not to make reply,
Theirs not to reason why,
Theirs but to do and die.
Into the valley of Death
   Rode the six hundred.

Cannon to right of them,
Cannon to left of them,
Cannon in front of them
   Volleyed and thundered;
Stormed at with shot and shell,
Boldly they rode and well,
Into the jaws of Death,
Into the mouth of Hell
   Rode the six hundred.

Flashed all the sabres bare,
Flashed as they turned in air
Sabring the gunners there,
Charging an army, while
   All the world wondered:
Plunged in the battery-smoke
Right through the line they broke;
Cossack and Russian
Reeled from the sabre-stroke
   Shattered and sundered.
Then they rode back, but not,
   Not the six hundred.

Cannon to right of them,
Cannon to left of them,
Cannon behind them
   Volleyed and thundered;
Stormed at with shot and shell,
While horse and hero fell,
That they had fought so well
Came through the jaws of Death,
Back from the mouth of Hell,
All that was left of them,
   Left of six hundred.

When can their glory fade?
O the wild charge they made!
    All the world wondered.
Honour the charge they made!
Honour the Light Brigade,
    Noble six hundred!

Alfred Lord Tennyson

Me and My Brother

Me and my brother,
we sit up in bed
doing my dad's sayings.
I go to bed first
and I'm just dozing off
and I hear a funny voice going:
'Never let me see you doing that again,'
and it's my brother
poking his finger out just like my dad
going:
'Never let me see you doing that again.'
And so I join in
and we're both going:
'Never let me see you doing that again.'
So what happens next time I get into trouble
and my dad's telling me off?
He's going:

'Never let me see you doing that again.'
So I'm looking up at my dad going,
'Sorry, Dad, sorry,'
and I suddenly catch sight of my brother's
   big red face
poking out from behind my dad.
And while my dad is poking me with his
   finger in time with the words:
'Never let me see you doing that again,'
there's my brother doing just the same
behind my dad's back
just where I can see him
and he's saying the words as well
with his mouth without making a sound.
So I start laughing
and so my dad says,
'AND IT'S NO LAUGHING MATTER.'
Of course my brother knows that one as well
and he's going with his mouth:
'And it's no laughing matter.'
But my dad's not stupid.
He knows something's going on.
So he looks round
and there's my brother
with his finger poking out
just like my dad
and I'm standing there laughing.
Oh no
then we get into
REALLY BIG TROUBLE.

Michael Rosen

The Apple-Raid

Darkness came early, though not yet cold;
Stars were strung on the telegraph wires;
Street lamps spilled pools of liquid gold;
The breeze was spiced with garden fires.

That smell of burnt leaves, the early dark,
Can still excite me but not as it did
So long ago when we met in the park –
Myself, John Peters and David Kidd.

We moved out of town to the district where
The lucky and wealthy had their homes
With garages, gardens, and apples to spare
Ripely clustered in the trees' green domes.

We chose the place we meant to plunder
And climbed the wall and dropped down to
The secret dark. Apples crunched under
Our feet as we moved through the grass and dew.

The clusters on the lower boughs of the tree
Were easy to reach. We stored the fruit
In pockets and jerseys until all three
Boys were heavy with their tasty loot.

Safe on the other side of the wall
We moved back to town and munched as we went.
I wonder if David remembers at all
That little adventure, the apples' fresh scent.

Strange to think that he's fifty years old,
That tough little boy with scabs on his knees;
Stranger to think that John Peters lies cold
In an orchard in France beneath apple trees.

Vernon Scannell

Conversations and Monologues

Conversations are made up of two or more voices.
Monologues are poems specifically written for one voice.
Usually they tell some sort of story.

The Dark Avenger
for 2 voices

My dog is called The Dark Avenger.
Hello, I'm Cuddles.

She understands every word I say.
Woof?

Last night I took her for a walk.
Woof! Walkies! Let's go!

Cleverly, she kept 3 paces ahead.
I dragged him along behind me.

She paused at every danger, spying out the land.
I stopped at every lamp-post.

When the coast was clear, she sped on.
I slipped my lead and ran away.

Scenting danger, Avenger investigated.
I found some fresh chip papers in the bushes.

I followed, every sense alert.
He blundered through the trees, shouting, 'Oy, Come 'ere!
Where are you?'

Something – maybe a sixth sense – told me to stop.
He tripped over me in the dark.

There was a pale menacing figure ahead of us.
Then I saw the white Scottie from next door.

Avenger sprang into battle, eager to defend his master.
Never could stand terriers!

They fought like tigers.
We scrapped like dogs.

Until the enemy was defeated.
Till Scottie's owner pulled him off – spoilsport!

Avenger gave a victory salute.
I rolled in the puddles.

And came to check I was all right.
I shook mud over him.

'Stop it, you stupid dog!'
He congratulated me.

Sometimes, even The Dark Avenger can go too far.
Woof!!

Trevor Millum

Two Witches Discuss Good Grooming

'How do you keep your teeth so green
Whilst mine remain quite white?
Although I rub them vigorously
With cold slime every night.

'Your eyes are such a lovely shade
Of bloodshot, streaked with puce.
I prod mine daily with a stick
But it isn't any use.

'I envy so, the spots and boils
That brighten your complexion.
Even rat spit on my face
Left no trace of infection.

'I've even failed to have bad breath
After eating sewage raw,
Yet your halitosis
Can strip paint from a door.'

'*My dear, there is no secret,*
Now I don't mean to brag.
What you see is nature's work,
I'm just a natural hag.'

John Coldwell

Conversation Piece

Late again, Blenkinsop?
What's the excuse this time?
Not my fault, sir.
Whose fault is it then?
Grandma's, sir.
Grandma's. What did she do?
She died, sir.
Died?
She's seriously dead all right, sir.
That makes four grandmothers this term
And all on PE days, Blenkinsop.
I know. It's very upsetting, sir.
How many grandmothers have you got, Blenkinsop?
Grandmothers, sir? None, sir.
None?
All dead, sir.
And what about yesterday, Blenkinsop?
What about yesterday, sir?
You missed maths.
That was the dentist, sir.
The dentist died?
No, sir. My teeth, sir.
You missed the test, Blenkinsop.
I'd been looking forward to it too, sir.
Right, line up for PE.
Can't, sir.
No such word as can't. Why can't you?
No kit, sir.

Where is it?
Home, sir.
What's it doing at home?
Not ironed, sir.
Couldn't you iron it?
Can't do it, sir.
Why not?
My hand, sir.
Who usually does it?
Grandma, sir.
Why couldn't she do it?
Dead, sir.

Gareth Owen

Conversation

I'm just going out for a moment.
Why?
To make a cup of tea.
Why?
Because I'm thirsty.
Why?
Because it's hot.
Why?
Because the sun's shining.
Why?
Because it's summer.
Why?
Because that's when it is.
Why?
Why don't you stop saying why?
Why?
Tea-time. That's why.
High-time-you-stopped-saying-why-time.
What?

Michael Rosen

The Lion and Albert

There's a famous seaside place called Blackpool,
That's noted for fresh air and fun,
And Mr and Mrs Ramsbottom
Went there with young Albert, their son.

A grand little lad was young Albert,
All dressed in his best; quite a swell
With a stick with an 'orse's 'ead 'andle,
The finest that Woolworth's could sell.

They didn't think much to the Ocean:
The waves, they was fiddlin' and small,
There was no wrecks and nobody drownded,
Fact, nothing to laugh at at all.

So, seeking for further amusement,
They paid and went into the Zoo,
Where they'd Lions and Tigers and Camels,
And old ale and sandwiches too.

There were one great big Lion called Wallace;
His nose were all covered with scars –
He lay in a somnolent posture,
With the side of his face on the bars.

Now Albert had heard about Lions,
How they was ferocious and wild –
To see Wallace lying so peaceful,
Well, it didn't seem right to the child.

So straightway the brave little feller,
Not showing a morsel of fear,
Took his stick with its 'orse's 'ead 'andle
And pushed it in Wallace's ear.

You could see that the Lion didn't like it,
For giving a kind of a roll,
He pulled Albert inside the cage with 'im,
And swallowed the little lad 'ole.

Then Pa, who had seen the occurrence,
And didn't know what to do next,
Said 'Mother! Yon Lion's 'et Albert',
And Mother said 'Well, I am vexed!'

Then Mr and Mrs Ramsbottom –
Quite rightly, when all's said and done –
Complained to the Animal Keeper,
That the Lion had eaten their son.

The keeper was quite nice about it;
He said 'What a nasty mishap.
Are you sure that it's *your* boy he's eaten?'
Pa said 'Am I sure? There's his cap!'

The manager had to be sent for.
He came and he said 'What's to do?'
Pa said 'Yon Lion's 'et Albert,
And 'im in his Sunday clothes, too.'

Then Mother said, 'Right's right, young feller;
I think it's a shame and a sin,
For a lion to go and eat Albert,
And after we've paid to come in.'

The manager wanted no trouble,
He took out his purse right away,
Saying 'How much to settle the matter?'
And Pa said 'What do you usually pay?'

But Mother had turned a bit awkward
When she thought where her Albert had gone.
She said 'No! someone's got to be summonsed' –
So that was decided upon.

Then off they went to the P'lice Station,
In front of the Magistrate chap;
They told 'im what happened to Albert,
And proved it by showing his cap.

The Magistrate gave his opinion
That no one was really to blame
And he said that he hoped the Ramsbottoms
Would have further sons to their name.

At that Mother got proper blazing,
'And thank you, sir, kindly,' said she.
'What waste all our lives raising children
To feed ruddy Lions? Not me!'

Marriott Edgar

All the World's a Stage

All the world's a stage,
And all the men and women merely players:
They have their exits and their entrances;
And one man in his time plays many parts,
His acts being seven ages. At first the infant,
Mewling and puking in the nurse's arms.
And then the whining schoolboy, with his satchel,
And shining morning face, creeping like snail
Unwilling to school. And then the lover,
Sighing like furnace, with a woeful ballad
Made to his mistress' eyebrow. Then a soldier,
Full of strange oaths, and bearded like the pard,
Jealous in honour, sudden and quick in quarrel,
Seeking the bubble reputation
Even in the cannon's mouth. And then the justice,
In fair round belly with good capon lin'd,
With eyes severe, and beard of formal cut,
Full of wise saws and modern instances;
And so he plays his part. The sixth age shifts

Into the lean and slipper'd pantaloon,
With spectacles on nose and pouch on side,
His youthful hose well sav'd, a world too wide
For his shrunk shank; and his big manly voice,
Turning again towards childish treble, pipes
And whistles in his sound. Last scene of all,
That ends this strange eventful history,
Is second childishness and mere oblivion,
Sans teeth, sans eyes, sans taste, sans everything.

from As You Like It *by William Shakespeare*

The Evacuee

With a label on my blazer
And a suitcase in my hand,
My gas mask slung across me,
Very frightened here I stand.

I can hear some children crying,
Others laughing, but not I,
For I'm waiting very quietly,
And feeling small and shy.

We've travelled on a chugging train,
We've travelled on a bus,
And now we're lined up in the street,
And told we musn't fuss.

And the teachers study names on lists,
And knock upon each door,
'Did you say you'd have one little girl?'
And 'Could you have one more?'

I haven't got a sister,
And I haven't got a brother,
And that is why they take me out
The first of any other.

But at tea-time Billy Brown's still there,
The twins are at his side,
They've got very dirty faces,
Where the tears have streaked and dried.

And I have the strangest feeling,
When I'm grown up, I'll remember,
This year of 1939,
The sad month of September.

And I'll think about the night-time,
When my mum was far away,
And hope that other children
Never know so long a day.

Shirley Tomlinson

Journey of the Magi

'A cold coming we had of it,
Just the worst time of the year
For a journey, and such a long journey:
The ways deep and the weather sharp,
The very dead of winter.'
And the camels galled, sore-footed, refractory,
Lying down in the melting snow.
There were times we regretted
The summer palaces on slopes, the terraces,
And the silken girls bringing sherbet.
Then the camel men cursing and grumbling
And running away, and wanting their liquor and women,
And the night-fires going out, and the lack of shelters,
And the cities hostile and the towns unfriendly
And the villages dirty and charging high prices:
A hard time we had of it.
At the end we preferred to travel all night,
Sleeping in snatches.
With the voices singing in our ears, saying
That this was all folly.
Then at dawn we came down to a temperate valley,
Wet, below the snow line, smelling of vegetation;
With a running stream and a water-mill beating the darkness,
And three trees on the low sky.
And an old white horse galloped away in the meadow.
Then we came to a tavern with vine-leaves over the lintel,
Six hands at an open door dicing for pieces of silver,
And feet kicking the empty wine-skins.

But there was no information, and so we continued
And arrived at evening, not a moment too soon
Finding the place; it was (you may say) satisfactory.

All this was a long time ago, I remember,
And I would do it again, but set down
This set down
This: were we led all that way for
Birth or Death? There was a Birth, certainly,
We had evidence and no doubt. I had seen birth and death,
But had thought they were different; this Birth was
Hard and bitter agony for us, like Death, our death.
We returned to our places, these Kingdoms,
But no longer at ease here, in the old dispensation,
With an alien people clutching their gods.
I should be glad of another death.

T. S. Eliot

Macbeth

Tomorrow, and tomorrow, and tomorrow,
Creeps in this petty pace from day to day,
To the last syllable of recorded time;
And all our yesterdays have lighted fools
The ways to dusty death. Out, out, brief candle,
Life's but a walking shadow, a poor player,
That struts and frets his hour upon the stage,
And then is heard no more: it is a tale
Told by an idiot, full of sound and fury,
Signifying nothing.

from Macbeth *by William Shakespeare*

Stopping by Woods on a Snowy Evening

Whose woods these are I think I know.
His house is in the village though;
He will not see me stopping here
To watch his woods fill up with snow.

My little horse must think it queer
To stop without a farmhouse near
Between the woods and frozen lake
The darkest evening of the year.

He gives his harness bells a shake
To ask if there is some mistake.
The only other sound's the sweep
Of easy wind and downy flake.

The woods are lovely, dark and deep,
But I have promises to keep,
And miles to go before I sleep,
And miles to go before I sleep.

Robert Frost

The Register

Right, Class 6
register time –
that means everyone sitting down.
Everyone, Darren.
No, Darren, we're not feeding the snails now.
Sarah, could you pass me the register?
No I haven't got it, you've got it.
You went to fetch it, remember?
Oh that was yesterday was it?
Darren, leave the snails alone.
One moment everyone, Mr Hardware wants a word.
Right, Class 6
Mr Hardware says that any tennis balls landing
in the gutter by the kitchen will be left there till

490

Christmas
when they'll be sent to Dr Barnardo's.
No, he's not my doctor, Louise
my doctor doesn't need tennis balls
Dr Barnardo's not alive he's –
I know, Wayne, that if he's not alive
he can't use the tennis balls.
Darren, don't touch the snails, do you hear me?
Does anyone know who or what is Dr Barnardo's?
No, Hugh, not a dog's home.
Yes, Abdul, a children's home, well done.
I wonder, Mrs Morris –
I don't want to be rude –
but I'm just settling the children down,
perhaps you could see a way to leaving now,
mmm?
I'm sure David is OK, Mrs Morris.
Yes, cake-making on Friday will be lovely, Mrs Morris
but –
Wayne that is very rude.
We've talked about kissing before.
If Mrs Morris wants to kiss David goodbye
that's OK and you've no right to laugh at –
thank you again, Mrs Morris, yes biscuit-making too
that'll be lovely, thank you so much,
goodbye, Mrs Morris,
she's not waving to you, Sophie.
Yes, Colin?
Well, I'm sure Mr Hardware means any kind of ball
footballs, basketballs.

You got a baseball from your American cousin.
That was very nice of him.
No I don't know who won the World Series.
I can't guess because I don't know the names
of any of the baseball teams.
Ah – Mrs Riley, good morning,
Right, Class 6
Mrs Riley says that if anyone who usually has school
dinner
on a Thursday but wants a school packed lunch for the
outing
to the Science Museum, then could they fill in the form.
Yes, Judy?
The form.
Well, I'm not quite sure what form for the moment
but I'm sure a form will be coming along soon.
They usually do.
And I'll tell you when it does.
Well, if you don't want a school packed lunch
and you don't bring a packed lunch
then you'll be very hungry, won't you?
Darren, I don't want to have to tell you about the snails
again
we're doing the register now, not snails,
Yes, Zoë I know quite well that I'm not actually doing the
register
at this very second
but, I will be
and I would be
and I could be . . .

Do you know what the time is, Mervyn?
You do.
Do you know how many minutes late you are, Mervyn?
You do.
Do you know why you're late every morning, Mervyn?
You do.
Do you have any idea how we are going to get you
to come to school on time, Mervyn?
You don't.
Mark and Hong are sitting very nicely.
Ah, Mrs Morris, you're back.
Yes, we could make toffee as well
an excellent idea . . .
Qui-et!
There'll be no toffee for anyone
if there's that kind of noise . . .
thank you so much, Mrs Morris
I'm sure we have the right pans for making toffee
but I can't look just now
bye bye yes of course, bye bye
Rasheda, Jason, Simone all sitting very nicely
Darren not sitting nicely.
Not sitting at all in fact.
Oh no he's left the lid off.
quick, Abdul
the lid
put the lid back on the snails.
What? One's missing.
Which one?
No not all of you.

Everyone come back,
sit down.
Abdul and just Abdul,
can you tell us which snail is missing?
Robin.
Was Robin in the aquarium before?
Darren?
No, Mervyn, snails don't eat each other.
You know they eat leaves.
All term we've been looking at how they eat leaves
we've written poems about how they eat leaves
we've drawn graphs of how many leaves they eat in a day
and now you're telling me that they eat each other.
You know sometimes I wonder why we've got these snails
here.
It really isn't anything to cry about, Paul.
I know Robin was your favourite
and I'm sure Batman doesn't miss him.
I'm not sure snails do miss each other.
Look, I don't want to deal with this just now.
I'm sure Robin will turn up,
he can't have gone far.
Snails don't gallop do they?
Darren, is that the truth?
Is what Salima is saying true?
Is it?
Well, take Robin out of your pocket right now,
put him back in the aquarium
and go straight downstairs to see Mrs Rashid
and you can explain to her what you did to Robin.

I'm not sure you'll be here for Mrs Morris's baking day
at this rate.
Ah who's this?
John.
No, I'm sorry, John you can't have the register
just yet.
Tell Mrs Riley we'll be down with it in just a moment.
Right, Class 6.
The register.
Oh – where is it?
It was here just a moment ago.
Can anyone see the register?
Can anyone see the register?

Michael Rosen

You're

Clownlike, happiest on your hands,
Feet to the stars, and moon-skulled,
Gilled like a fish. A common-sense
Thumbs down on the dodo's mode.
Wrapped up in yourself like a spool,
Trawling your dark as owls do,
Mute as a turnip from the Fourth
Of July to All Fool's day,
O high-riser, my little loaf.

Vague as fog and looked for like mail,
Farther off than Australia.
Bent-backed Atlas, our travelled prawn.
Snug as bud and at home
Like a sprat in a pickle jug.
A creel of eels, all ripples.
Jumpy as a Mexican bean.
Right, like a well-done sum.
A clean slate, with your own face on.

Sylvia Plath

Stage Directions for Bluebells

OK. Everyone else off-stage –
we'll just have bluebells for this one.
Lilac? Don't fire your torches yet.
Daisies? Just stay folded, will you?
Now. Bluebells. Can we all be up-
standing? That's it. Spread yourselves
about a bit. Use the whole stage.
What d'you think we've got all this green
foliage for? Nice! Nice! Now families –
over on the right, please. And you two –
could you appear to be in conversation,
or at least on nodding acquaintance? No,
there's no need to be facetious. You don't
have to ring. Solitaries? Nestle in the shade

496

among the ferns and ivies. No, you can't
have extra lighting. It's contrast we're after.
OK. You shy, flirty ones – over by the wall.
Peep through the peonies. Can you tremble?
Very nice! Miss Precocious? By the rose.
Now. You extras. All right, all righty,
individuals. We're running out of space here.
Do what you can with the cracks in the path.
Yes, I realize you might get trampled on –
that's just a risk you've got to take.
Lovely! Lovely! You all look very picturesque.
OK. That's it! Hold it! Hold it!
We'll call it 'Late April in England, with
  bluebells'.

Dinah Hendry

No-Speaks

I am the child who stopped talking
Three years ago. There was heavy snow.
It was a blow to my family, I know.
They call me No-Speaks.
It has been one hundred and fifty-six weeks
Since I came to the decision about speech.
I clocked it was a waste of time,
to talk in plain speech or rhyme.
So, I watch the telling hands chime.
I watch the trees grow big beards, fuzzy hair.
Then, I watch them get alopecia.
I watch the snow melt into summer.
I hold my tongue round the clock.
The call me No-Speaks.
I shut my mouth from season to season.
I have a very good reason
For never saying a single word.
Not a single dickie bird.
(I was not struck by lightning.
I did not witness something shocking.)
(If two people tell the same lie
at the same time, one will die
Before the year is over.)
My lips are sealed, January to December.
They call me No-Speaks.
I am a closed book. A sealed letter.
A shut letter-box.
I despise the blether, the chatterbox.

Since I shut my trap,
Life is much better.
But every sound is an electric shock.
Leaves are shy when they first
fall from trees.

                              Jackie Kay

Fighting the Tide

On holidays, after seven and a half months
of counting the days since Christmas
(Easter is good – but there's only
so much fun in chocolate eggs),
after the excited sing-song journey
and me being sick, 'Every twenty miles!'
according to my dad,
we would go to the beach every day of the fortnight
and eat sandy sandwiches,
packets of family-size crisps – each,
swig Coke.
stuff 99s,
and each a whole chicken, or ham,
or at the end of the fortnight, a tin of spam,
between us.
The rest ate whole tomatoes,
(but not me, I don't like them –
'Fussy eater', my nan says).

But my favourite part of every day was
fighting the tide.
My sister, my brother and I would build
huge walls of sand,
defences against the battery of the tide's attack.
The design would change every time with
each of us arguing whether a pointed end would
stay standing longer than a rounded wall.
There was no time to decorate these sea walls
with castellations or crenellations,
towers or gates.

The onslaught of the tide was there to be fought.
We lost.
Every day.
But every day
we fought
just the same.

In the evening we would sit in the bar with the adults
fighting the tide of sleep.

At the end of the fortnight, I would fight the tide of leaving.

Part of me is always with my brother and sister, fighting
    the tide.

Huw James

Night Light

When I was small
each night
was a bottomless ocean.
But I had a pale pink
plastic lighthouse
with a one-watt bulb,
enough to tip its wink
to the brass of the doorknob
like a ship
passing far out to sea.
And high above it all
on a safe shore
was the lookout: me.

And now
I'm told that space
is truly bottomless
and endless and the sun
is a tiny nightlight
glinting sometimes
on nine crumbs
of rock or ice
and there's nowhere anyone
can stand above it all.
Hello? Can anybody
hear me? I'm
so small.

Philip Gross

Classic Poems

These are poems by well-known poets from the past that have stood the test of time and are therefore generally acknowledged to be great and valuable pieces of writing.

From a Railway Carriage

Faster than fairies, faster than witches,
Bridges and houses, hedges and ditches;
And charging along like troops in a battle,
All through the meadows the horses and cattle:
All of the sights of the hill and the plain
Fly as thick as driving rain;
And ever again, in the wink of an eye,
Painted stations whistle by.

Here is a child who clambers and scrambles,
All by himself and gathering brambles;
Here is a tramp who stands and gazes;
And there is the green for stringing the daisies!
Here is a cart run away in the road
Lumping along with man and load;
And here is a mill, and there is a river:
Each a glimpse and gone for ever!

Robert Louis Stevenson

If

If you can keep your head when all about you
Are losing theirs and blaming it on you,
If you can trust yourself when all men doubt you,
But make allowance for their doubting too;
If you can wait and not be tired of waiting,
Or being lied about, don't deal in lies,
Or being hated, don't give way to hating,
And yet don't look too good, nor talk too wise:

If you can dream – and not make dreams your master;
If you can think – and not make thoughts your aim;
If you can meet with Triumph and Disaster
And treat those two impostors just the same;
If you can bear to hear the truth you've spoken
Twisted by knaves to make a trap for fools,
Or watch the things you gave your life to, broken,
And stoop and build 'em up with worn-out tools:

If you can make one heap of all your winnings
And risk it on the turn of pitch-and-toss,
And lose, and start again at your beginnings
And never breathe a word about your loss;
If you can force your heart and nerve and sinew
To serve your turn long after they are gone,
And so hold on when there is nothing in you
Except the Will which says to them: 'Hold on!'

If you can talk with crowds and keep your virtue,
Or walk with Kings – nor lose the common touch,
If neither foes nor loving friends can hurt you,
If all men count with you, but none too much;
If you can fill the unforgiving minute
With sixty seconds' worth of distance run,
Yours is the Earth and everything that's in it,
And – which is more – you'll be a Man, my son!

Rudyard Kipling

The Road Not Taken

Two roads diverged in a yellow wood,
And sorry I could not travel both
And be one traveller, long I stood
And looked down one as far as I could
To where it bent in the undergrowth;

Then took the other, as just as fair,
And having perhaps the better claim,
Because it was grassy and wanted wear;
Though as for that the passing there
Had worn them really about the same,

And both that morning equally lay
In leaves no step had trodden black.
Oh, I kept the first for another day!
Yet knowing how way leads on to way,
I doubted if I should ever come back.

I shall be telling this with a sigh
Somewhere ages and ages hence:
Two roads diverged in a wood, and I –
I took the one less travelled by,
And that has made all the difference.

Robert Frost

To Autumn

Seasons of mists and mellow fruitfulness,
  Close bosom-friend of the maturing sun,
Conspiring with him how to load and bless
  With fruit the vines that round the thatch-eaves run;
To bend with apples the mossed cottage-trees,
  And fill all fruit with ripeness to the core;
    To swell the gourd, and plum the hazel shells
With a sweet kernel; to set budding more,
  And still more, later flowers for the bees,
  Until they think warm days will never cease,
    For summer has o'er-brimmed their clammy cells.

Who hath not seen thee oft amid thy store?
    Sometimes whoever seeks abroad may find
Thee sitting careless on a granary floor,
    Thy hair soft-lifted by the winnowing wind;
Or on a half-reaped furrow sound asleep,
    Drowsed with the fumes of poppies, while thy hook
        Spares the next swath and all its twined flowers;
And sometimes like a gleaner thou dost keep
    Steady thy laden head across a brook;
Or by a cider-press, with patient look,
        Thou watchest the last oozings hours by hours.

Where are the songs of spring? Aye, where are they?
    Think not of them, thou hast thy music too –
While barred clouds bloom the soft-dying day,
    And touch the stubble-plains with rosy hue;
Then in a wailful choir the small gnats mourn
    Among the river sallows, borne aloft
        Or sinking, as the light wind lives or dies;
And full-grown lambs loud bleat from hilly bourn;
    Hedge-crickets sing; and now with treble soft
The redbreast whistles from a garden-croft;
        And gathering swallows twitter in the skies.

John Keats

Ozymandias

I met a traveller from an antique land
Who said: Two vast and trunkless legs of stone
Stand in the desert. Near them, on the sand,
Half sunk, a shattered visage lies, whose frown,
And wrinkled lip, and sneer of cold command
Tell that its sculptor well those passions read
Which yet survive (stamped on these lifeless things)
The hand that mocked them and the heart that fed:
And on the pedestal these words appear:
'My name is Ozymandias, King of Kings:
Look on my works, ye Mighty, and despair!'
Nothing beside remains. Round the decay
Of that colossal wreck, boundless and bare
The lone and level sands stretch far away.

Percy Bysshe Shelley

Sonnet

Remember me when I am gone away.
  Gone far away into the silent land:
  When you can no more hold me by the hand,
Nor I half turn to go yet turning stay.
Remember me when no more day by day
  You tell me of our future that you planned:
  Only remember me; you understand
It will be late to counsel then or pray.
Yet if you should forget me for a while
  And afterwards remember, do not grieve:
  For if the darkness and corruption leave
  A vestige of the thoughts that once I had,
Better by far that you should forget and smile
  Than that you should remember and be sad.

Christina Rossetti

Eldorado

Gaily bedight,
A gallant knight,
In sunshine and in shadow,
Had journeyed long,
Singing a song,
In search of Eldorado.

But he grew old –
This knight so bold –
And o'er his heart a shadow
Fell as he found
No spot of ground
That looked like Eldorado.

And, as his strength
Failed him at length,
He met a pilgrim shadow:
'Shadow,' said he,
'Where can it be,
This land of Eldorado?'

'Over the mountains
Of the Moon,
Down the valley of the Shadow,
Ride, boldly ride,'
The shade replied,
'If you seek for Eldorado.'

Edgar Allen Poe

How Do I Love Thee?

How do I love thee? Let me count the ways,
I love thee to the depth and breadth and height
My soul can reach, when feeling out of sight
For the ends of Being and ideal Grace.

I love thee to the level of everyday's
Most quiet need, by sun and candlelight.
I love thee freely, as men strive for Right;
I love thee purely, as they turn from Praise.

I love thee with the passion put to use
In my old griefs, and with my childhood's faith.
I love thee with a love I seemed to lose

With my lost saints – I love thee with the breath,
Smiles, tears, of all my life! – and, if God choose
I shall but love thee better after death.

Elizabeth Barrett Browning

Daffodils

I wander'd lonely as a cloud
  That floats on high o'er vales and hills,
When all at once I saw a crowd,
  A host of golden daffodils;
Beside the lake, beneath the trees,
Fluttering and dancing in the breeze.

Continuous as the stars that shine
  And twinkle on the Milky Way,
They stretch'd in never-ending line
  Along the margin of a bay:
Ten thousand saw I at a glance,
Tossing their heads in sprightly dance.

The waves beside them danced, but they
  Out-did the sparkling waves in glee:
A poet could not but be gay,
  In such a jocund company:
I gazed – and gazed – but little thought
What wealth the show to me had brought:

For oft, when on my couch I lie
  In vacant or in pensive mood,
They flash upon that inward eye
  Which is the bliss of solitude;
And then my heart with pleasure fills,
And dances with the daffodils.

William Wordsworth

A Red, Red Rose

O, my Luve's like a red, red rose,
    That's newly sprung in June.
O, my Luve's like the melodie
    That's sweetly play'd in tune.

As fair art thou, my bonnie lass,
    So deep in luve am I;
And I will love thee still, my dear.
    Till a' the seas gang dry.

Till a' the seas gang dry, my dear,
    And the rocks melt wi' the sun:
I will love thee still, my dear,
    While the sands o' life shall run:

And fare thee weel, my only luve!
    And fare thee weel, a while!
And I will come again, my luve,
    Tho' it ware ten thousand mile!

Robert Burns

Upon Westminster Bridge

Earth has not anything to show more fair:
Dull would he be of soul who could pass by
A sight so touching in its majesty:
This City now doth, like a garment, wear
The beauty of the morning; silent, bare,
Ships, towers, domes, theatres, and temples lie
Open unto the fields, and to the sky;
All bright and glittering in the smokeless air.
Never did sun more beautifully steep
In his first splendour, valley, rock, or hill;
Ne'er saw I, never felt, a calm so deep!
The river glideth at his own sweet will:
Dear God! the very houses seem asleep;
And all the mighty heart is lying still!

William Wordsworth

Funeral Blues

Stop all the clocks, cut off the telephone,
Prevent the dog from barking with a juicy bone,
Silence the pianos and with muffled drum
Bring out the coffin, let the mourners come.

Let aeroplanes circle moaning overhead
Scribbling on the sky the message He is Dead.
Put crêpe bows round the white necks of the public doves,
Let the traffic policemen wear black cotton gloves.

He was my North, my South, my East and West,
My working week and my Sunday rest,
My noon, my midnight, my talk, my song;
I thought that love would last for ever: I was wrong.

The stars are not wanted now: put out every one,
Pack up the moon and dismantle the sun,
Pour away the ocean and sweep up the wood;
For nothing now can ever come to any good.

W. H. Auden

Macavity: The Mystery Cat

Macavity's a Mystery Cat: he's called the Hidden Paw –
For he's the master criminal who can defy the Law.
He's the bafflement of Scotland Yard, the Flying Squad's
    despair:
For when they reach the scene of crime – *Macavity's not
    there!*

Macavity, Macavity, there's no one like Macavity,
He's broken every human law, he breaks the law of gravity.
His powers of levitation would make a fakir stare,
And when you reach the scene of crime – *Macavity's not there!*
You may seek him in the basement, you may look up in the air –
But I tell you once and once again, *Macavity's not there!*

Macavity's a ginger cat, he's very tall and thin;
You would know him if you saw him, for his eyes are sunken in.
His brow is deeply lined with thought, his head is highly domed;
His coat is dusty from neglect, his whiskers are uncombed.
He sways his head from side to side, with movements like a snake;
And when you think he's half asleep, he's always wide awake.

Macavity, Macavity, there's no one like Macavity,
For he's a fiend in feline shape, a monster of depravity.
You may meet him in a by-street, you may see him in the square –
But when a crime's discovered, then *Macavity's not there!*

He's outwardly respectable. (They say he cheats at cards.)
And his footprints are not found in any file of Scotland
　Yard's.
And when the larder's looted, or the jewel-case is rifled,
Or when the milk is missing, or another Peke's been stifled,
Or the greenhouse glass is broken, and the trellis past repair –
Ay, there's the wonder of the thing! *Macavity's not there!*

And when the Foreign Office find a Treaty's gone astray,
Or the Admiralty lose some plans and drawings by the way,
There may be a scrap of paper in the hall or on the stair –
But it's useless to investigate – *Macavity's not there!*
And when the loss has been disclosed, the Secret Service say:
'It *must* have been Macavity!' – but he's a mile away.
You'll be sure to find him resting, or a-licking of his thumbs,
Or engaged in doing complicated long division sums.

Macavity, Macavity, there's no one like Macavity,
There never was a Cat of such deceitfulness and suavity.
He always has an alibi, and one or two to spare:
At whatever time the deed took place – MACAVITY WASN'T
　THERE!
And they say that all the Cats whose wicked deeds are
　widely known
(I might mention Mungojerrie, I might mention
　Griddlebone)
Are nothing more than agents for the Cat who all the time
Just controls their operations: the Napoleon of Crime!

T. S. Eliot

Night Mail

This is the night mail crossing the border,
Bringing the cheque and the postal order,
Letters for the rich, letters for the poor,
The shop at the corner and the girl next door.
Pulling up Beattock, a steady climb –
The gradient's against her, but she's on time.

Past cotton grass and moorland boulder
Shovelling white steam over her shoulder,
Snorting noisily as she passes
Silent miles of wind-bent grasses.
Birds turn their heads as she approaches,
Stare from the bushes at her blank-faced coaches.
Sheepdogs cannot turn her course,
They slumber on with paws across.
In the farm she passes no one wakes,
But the jug in the bedroom gently shakes.

Dawn freshens, the climb is done
Down towards Glasgow she descends
Towards the steam tugs yelping down the glade of cranes,
Towards the fields of apparatus, the furnaces
Set on the dark plain like gigantic chessmen.
All Scotland waits for her:
In the dark glens, beside the pale-green lochs
Men long for news.

Letters of thanks, letters from banks,
Letters of joy from girl and boy,
Receipted bills and invitations
To inspect new stock or visit relations,
And applications for situations
And timid lovers' declarations
And gossip, gossip from all the nations,
News circumstantial, news financial.
Letters with holiday snaps to enlarge in,
Letters with faces scrawled in the margin,
Letters from uncles, cousins and aunts,
Letters to Scotland from the South of France,
Letters of condolence to Highlands and Lowlands,
Notes from overseas to Hebrides –
Written on paper of every hue,
The pink, the violet, the white and the blue,
The chatty, the catty, the boring, adoring,
The cold and official and the heart's outpouring,
Clever, stupid, short and long,
The typed and the printed and the spelt all wrong.
Thousands are still asleep
Dreaming of terrifying monsters,
Of a friendly tea beside the band at Cranston's or
   Crawford's:
Asleep in working Glasgow, asleep in well-set Edinburgh,
Asleep in granite Aberdeen.
They continue their dreams;
But shall wake soon and long for letters,
And none will hear the postman's knock

Without a quickening of the heart,
For who can hear and feel himself forgotten?

W. H. Auden

from *The Lady of Shalott*

I

On either side the river lie
Long fields of barley and of rye,
That clothe the wold and meet the sky;
And thro' the field the road runs by
   To many-tower'd Camelot;
And up and down the people go,
Gazing where the lilies blow
Round an island there below,
   The island of Shalott.

Willows whiten, aspens quiver,
Little breezes dusk and shiver
Thro' the wave that runs for ever
By the island in the river
   Flowing down to Camelot.
Four gray walls, and four gray towers,
Overlook a space of flowers,
And the silent isle imbowers
   The Lady of Shalott.

By the margin, willow-veil'd,
Slide the heavy barges trail'd
By slow horses; and unhail'd
The shallop flitteth silken-sail'd
    Skimming down to Camelot:
But who hath seen her wave her hand?
Or at the casement seen her stand?
Or is she known in all the land,
    The Lady of Shalott?

Only reapers, reaping early
In among the bearded barley,
Hear a song that echoes cheerly
From the river winding clearly,
    Down to tower'd Camelot:
And by moon the reaper weary,
Piling sheaves in uplands airy,
Listening, whispers, ''Tis the fairy
    Lady of Shalott.'

II

There she weaves by night and day
A magic web with colours gay.
She has heard a whisper say,
A curse is on her if she stay
　　To look down to Camelot.
She knows not what the curse may be,
And so she weaveth steadily,
And little other care hath she,
　　The Lady of Shalott.

And moving thro' a mirror clear
That hangs before her all the year,
Shadows of the world appear.
There she sees the highway near
　　Winding down to Camelot:
There the river eddy whirls,
And there the surly village-churls,
And the red cloaks of market girls,
　　Pass onward from Shalott.

Sometimes a troop of damsels glad,
An abbot on an ambling pad,
Sometimes a curly shepherd-lad,
Or long-hair'd page in crimson clad,
  Goes by to tower'd Camelot;
And sometimes thro' the mirror blue
The knights come riding two and two:
She hath no loyal knight and true,
  The Lady of Shalott.

But in her web she still delights
To weave the mirror's magic sights,
For often thro' the silent nights
A funeral, with plumes and lights,
  And music, went to Camelot:
Or when the moon was overhead,
Came two young lovers lately wed;
'I am half sick of shadows,' said
  The Lady of Shalott.

Alfred Lord Tennyson

Index of First Lines

Index of First Lines

Index of Poets

Index of Poets

Acknowledgements

The publishers wish to thank the following for permission to use copyright material:

John Agard, 'Who is de Girl?' from *No Hickory, No Dickory, No Dock*, Viking (1991), by permission of Caroline Sheldon Literary Agency on behalf of the author; **Allan Ahlberg**, 'Things I Have Been Doing Lately' from *Heard it in the Playground*, Viking (1989), p. 46. Copyright © Allan Ahlberg, 1989, by permission of Penguin UK; **W. H. Auden**, 'Twelve Songs IX' (Stop all the clocks . . ., here 'Funeral Blues') and 'Night Mail' from *Collected Poems by W. H. Auden*, by permission of Faber and Faber; **Leo Aylen**, 'Somewhere in the Sky' from *Rhymoceros*, Macmillan Children's Books (1989) and 'Riddle'; **Bruce Barnes**, 'I Wrote Me a Poem', first published in *Join In . . . Or Else*, Macmillan Children's Books, by permission of the author; **Basho**, 6 haiku from *On Love and Barley: Haiku of Basho*, translated by Lucien Stryk, Penguin Classics (1985), pp. 27, 30, 32, 33, 35. Copyright © Lucien Stryk, 1985, by permission of Penguin UK; **Les Baynton**, 'The Poetry United Chant', by permission of the author; **Hilaire Belloc**, 'Matilda' from *Complete Verse*, Pimlico. Copyright © The Estate of Hilaire Belloc, 1970, by permission of The Peters Fraser and Dunlop Group Ltd on behalf of the Estate of the author; **James Berry**, 'Duppy Dance', first published in *Unzip Your Lips*, Macmillan Children's Books, by permission of the author; **Tracey Blance**, 'School Trip' and 'I don't know what to write', by permission of the author; **Valerie Bloom**, 'Pinda Cake', 'Proverb', 'Haircut Rap', 'Cinquain', 'Fruits', 'Daddy's Gone to Market', 'Granny's in the Kitchen', 'Fishes in the River' and 'A-Gallop . . .', by permission of the author; **Dave Calder**, 'Pyramid', by permission of the author; **Richard Caley**, 'A Bedtime Prayer', 'Riddle – What am I?', 'Postcard from School Camp' and 'Somersault', by permission of the author; **James Carter**, 'The Shape I'm In' from *Creating Writers: A Creative Writing Manual for Schools*, Falmer (2000) and 'Dennis', by permission of the author; **Charles Causley**, 'Python on Piccolo', 'I am the Song', '"Quack!" said the Billy-goat' and 'Good Morning, Mr Croco-Doco-Dile' from *Collected Poems for Children*, Macmillan Children's Books, by permission of David Higham Associates on behalf of the author; **Debjani Chatterjee**, 'Proverbial Logic' first published in *Albino Gecko*, University of Salzburg Press, and 'Diwali', first published in *Unzip Your Lips Again!*, Macmillan Children's Books, by permission of the author; **Alison Chisolm**, 'About Knees', by permission of the author; **John Coldwell**, 'Dear Mrs Spider', 'Two Witches Discuss Good Grooming', 'William the Conqueror Sends a Postcard Home' and 'Wrestling with Mum', by permission of the author; **Andrew Collett**, 'Trainee Witch Wanted', 'Skip' and 'In the Bath', by permission of the author; **Paul Cookson**, 'It's Not The Same Any More' and 'These Are The Hands' from *Sing That Joke*, Solway Publishers (1998), 'Where Teachers Keep Their Pets' from *Teacher's Pets*,

Acknowledgements

Macmillan Children's Books (1999), 'Sea Shoals See Shows On The Sea Bed' and 'Billy Doesn't Like School Really' from *Elephant Dreams*, Macmillan Children's Books, 'Epitaph For The Last Martian' from *Aliens Stole My Underpants*, Macmillan Children's Books, 'Let No One Steal Your Dreams' from *Let No-one Steal Your Dreams*, 'Short Visit, Long Stay' from *Larks With Sharks*, Macmillan Children's Books, 'Picnic Time On The M25' from *Spill The Beans*, Macmillan Children's Books, 'Barry And Beryl The Bubble Gum Blowers' from *Tongue Twisters and Tonsil Twizzlers*, Macmillan Children's Books, 'The Skipping Rope Queen', 'Adelaide Crapsey', 'Edmund', 'The Model We're Making In Class With Miss', 'Teacher' and 'A Superhero Sends A Letter Home' by permission of the author; **John Cooper Clarke**, 'Haiku – To convey one's mood . . .', by permission of the author; **Pie Corbett**, 'Animal Riddle', 'A Poem To Be Spoken Quietly' and 'Wings', by permission of the author; **John Cotton**, 'Shadow' and 'April', by permission of the author; **Sue Cowling**, 'The First Diary', 'In Memoriam', 'Five Lines for Hallowe'en', 'Locker Inspection', 'Dandelion Time', 'Penguin', 'How Fire Came to Earth', 'Thank You Letters' and 'Spring Cleaning', by permission of the author; **June Crebbin**, 'Inside the Morning' and 'Making the Countryside' from *Cows Moo, Cars Toot!* by June Crebbin, Viking (1995), pp. 28, 29. Copyright (c) June Crebbin, 1991, by permission of Penguin UK; **Roald Dahl**, 'Little Red Riding Hood' from *Revolting Rhymes*, Jonathan Cape/Penguin Books, by permission of David Higham Associates on behalf of the Estate of the author; **Carmen Bernos de Gasztold**, 'The Prayer of the Cat' from *Prayers from the Ark*, translated by Rumer Godden, 1963, by permission of Macmillan Children's Books; **Walter de la Mare**, 'The Listeners' and 'Epitaph' from *The Complete Poems of Walter de la Mare*, 1969, by permission of the Literary Trustees of the author and The Society of Authors as their representative; **Emily Dickinson**, 'Bee! I'm Expecting You' from *The Poems of Emily Dickinson*, ed. Thomas H Johnson, The Belknap Press of Harvard University Press. Copyright © 1951, 1955, 1979, 1983 by the President and Fellows of Harvard College, by permission of the publishers and the Trustees of Amherst College; **Peter Dixon**, 'Magic Cat', 'Summer', 'Where Do All The Teachers Go?', 'Before the Days of Noah' and 'Marmalade', by permission of the author; **Gina Douthwaite**, 'Night Mer', by permission of the author; **Helen Dunmore**, 'Hedgehog Hiding at Harvest in Hills Above Monmouth' from *Secrets*, Bodley Head, by permission of A P Watt Ltd on behalf of the author; **George Marriott Edgar**, 'The Lion and Albert'. Copyright © 1933, by permission of EMI Music Publishing Ltd on behalf of Francis Day & Hunter Ltd; **Richard Edwards**, 'Some Favourite Words', by permission of the author; **T.S.Eliot**, 'The Song of the Jellicles' and 'Macavity: The Mystery Cat' from *Old Possum's Book of Practical Cats*. Copyright (c) 1939 by T. S. Eliot and renewed 1967 by Esme Valerie Eliot; and 'Journey of the Magi' from *Collected Poems 1909-1962*, by permission of Faber and Faber Ltd; **Malick Fall**, 'Empty Head' ('La Tête Vide') from *Reliefs*, Présence Africaine (1964), by permission of Présence Africaine: **Eleanor Farjeon**, 'A Morning Song', 'The Bonfire', 'Robin Hood' and 'Pegasus' from *Blackbird Has Spoken*, Macmillan

Acknowledgements

Children's Books, by permission of David Higham Associates on behalf of the Estate of the author; **John Foster**, 'Haiku – Bright as Butterflies', 'Acrostics', 'Dead End', 'Count Dracula', 'Children's Prayer', 'Neil Armstrong', 'Riddle', 'Here is the Seed', 'Diamond Poem', 'Silver Aeroplane', 'It's Spring', 'Leap like a Leopard', 'One for the Cluck of an Angry Hen', 'Wordspinning' and 'The Morning Rush'. Copyright (c) 2000 John Foster, by permission of the author; **Robert Frost**, 'The Road Not Taken' and 'Stopping by Woods on a Snowy Evening' from *The Poetry of Robert Frost*, ed. Edward Connery Lathem, Jonathan Cape, by permission of Random House UK; **Andrew Fusek Peters**, 'Five Little Senses All in a Row', by permission of the author; **Martin Glynn**, 'Wurd Up', 'Barefoot' and 'Genius', by permission of the author; **Gus Grenfell**, 'Cinquain – Come on you blues . . .' and 'My Brother', by permission of the author; **David Greygoose**, 'The Farmer's Cat', after a translation by Xia Lu, by permission of the author; **Philip Gross**, 'Night Line' from *The All-Nite Cafe*, by permission of Faber and Faber Ltd; **David Harmer**, 'Mister Moore', 'Who is My Neighbour?', 'Slick Nick's Dog Does Tricks', 'There's a Monster in the Garden', 'All Of Us Knocking On The Stable Door', 'My Mum's Put Me On The Transfer List', 'Uphill' and 'Dinner Lady', by permission of the author; **Trevor Harvey**, 'Rhythm Machine', first published in *Our Side of the Playground*, Bodley Head (1991) and 'My Eyes Are Watering', first published in *Word Whirls*, Oxford University Press (1998), by permission of the author; **John Hegley**, 'My Glasses' from *Glad to Wear Glasses* by John Hegley, Andre Deutsch (1990) and 'Emergensea' from *Love Cuts*, Methuen (1996), by permission of Peters Fraser and Dunlop Group Ltd on behalf of the author; **Diana Hendry**, 'Strange Directions for Bluebells', from *Strange Goings On* by Diana Hendry, Viking (1995). Copyright © Diana Hendry 1995, by permission of Rogers Coleridge & White Ltd on behalf of the author; **Adrian Henri**, 'Four Seasons Haiku', 'Nohaiku' and 'What Are Little Girls . . .' from *Robocat* (1998), by permission of Eunice McMullen Children's Literary Agency on behalf of the author; **Libby Houston** 'Shop Chat' from *Cover of Darkness, Selected Poems 1961-1998*, Slow Dancer Press, by permission of the author; **Ping Hsin**, 'Of Poets I Speak' from *Modern Chinese* Poetry, translated by Julia Lin, by permission of University of Washington Press; **Ted Hughes**, 'Amulet' and 'Mooses' from *Under the North Star* by Ted Hughes, and 'My Brother Bert' from *Meet My Folks!*, by permission of Faber and Faber Ltd; **John Irwin**, 'Fantastic Facts' and 'A Limerick's Cleverly Versed', by permission of the author; **Huw James**, 'Fighting the Tide', first published in *The Poets House*, ed. Jude Brigley, Pont Books (2000), by permission of the author; **Elizabeth Jennings**, 'For My Mother' from *Spell Of Words*, Macmillan Children's Books, by permission of David Higham Associates on behalf of the author; **Mike Johnson**, 'The Caractacus Chariot Company', by permission of the author; **Mike Jubb**, 'Cool Cat' and 'Camilla Caterpillar', by permission of the author; **Jackie Kay**, 'Word of a Lie' and 'No-Speaks' from *The Frog who Dreamed she was an Opera Singer* (1998), by permission of Bloomsbury Publishing; **Rudyard**

Acknowledgements

Kipling, 'If' and 'A Smuggler's Song' by permission of A P Watt Ltd on behalf of The National Trust for Places of Historic Interest or Natural Beauty; **John Kitching**, 'Round and Round', 'The pen in my . . .', 'Oystered haiku words . . .', 'The shell on my . . .'; 'Tanka 1', 'Tanka 2', 'I'm Free', 'Letter To An Unknown Father', 'Napoleon Bonaparte' and an extract from 'Family Problems', by permission of the author; **Naoshi Koriyama**, 'Unfolding Bud', first appeared in *The Christian Science Monitor*, 3.7.57. Copyright © The Christian Science Publishing Society, by permission of The Christian Science Publishing Society; **Patricia Leighton**, 'Introducing the . . .', by permission of the author; **Anne Logan**, 'The Yo-yo Man', by permission of the author; **Rupert Loydell**, 'Prayer', by permission of the author; **Wes Magee**, 'At the End of a School Day' and 'A Who'Z Who of the Horrible House', by permission of the author; **Gerda Mayer**, 'Shallow Poem' from *The Knockabout Show* by Gerda Mayer, Chatto & Windus (1978), by permission of the author; **Kevin McCann**, 'New School', by permission of the author; **Roger McGough**, 'Jane Austen' from *Nailing the Shadow*, Puffin (1987), 'The Sound Collector' from *Pillow Talk*, 'An Acrostic' from *Crack Another Yolk*, 'Haiku' and 'Poem for a Dead Poet'. Copyright © Roger McGough, by permission of Peters Fraser and Dunlop Group Ltd on behalf of the author; **Ian McMillan**, 'Can't Be Bothered to Think of a Title', 'Ten Things Found in a Wizard's Pocket', 'An Interesting Fact About One of My Relatives' and 'Counting the Stars', by permission of the author; **Spike Milligan**, 'On the Ning Nang Nong', by permission of Spike Milligan Productions Ltd; **Trevor Millum**, 'The Dark Avenger', first published in *Double Talk* by Trevor Millum and Bernard Young, 'Dick's Dog', 'Jabbermockery', 'Younger Brother' and 'Sunday in the Yarm Fard', by permission of the author; **Adrian Mitchell**, 'Patchwork Rap' from *Balloon Lagoon and The Magic Islands of Poetry*, Orchard Books (1997), and 'Yes'. Copyright © Adrian Mitchell, by permission of Peters Fraser and Dunlop Group Ltd on behalf of the author; **Tony Mitton**, 'Willow Pattern' from *Plum*, 'Write-a-Rap Rap', 'Things I'd Do If It Weren't For Mum', 'Things I'd Do If It Weren't For My Son', 'Teaser', 'Undersea Tea', 'Thunderbird', 'Where to put your poem' and 'The Bug Chant'. Copyright © Tony Mitton 2000, by permission of David Higham Associates on behalf of the author; **Michaela Morgan**, 'A to Z', by permission of the author; **Brian Moses**, 'What Teachers Wear in Bed' and 'Aliens Stole My Underpants', by permission of the author; **Judith Nicholls**, 'Have You Read?', 'How the Tortoise got its Shell', 'The Lion and the Mouse', 'Song of the Kite', 'Jack's Tale', 'Spring Magic', 'Explosive Tale', 'Future Past', 'B, beautiful B', 'Breakfast for One' and 'Skipping Rhyme'. Copyright © 2000 Judith Nicholls, by permission of the author; **Grace Nichols**, 'Give Yourself a Hug' from *Give Yourself a Hug*, A & C Black (1994) and 'Baby-K Rap Rhyme' from *No Hickory No Dickory No Dock*. Copyright © Grace Nichols 1991, 1994, by permission of Curtis Brown Ltd, London, on behalf of the author; **Alfred Noyes**, 'The Highwayman' from *Collected Poems*, by permission of John Murray (Publishers) Ltd; **David Orme**, 'Teacher's Day in Bed' and 'An Old Cat

Acknowledgements

is Annoyed by a Dove', by permission of the author; **Jack Ousbey**, 'Gran, Can You Rap?', first published in *All in the Family*, collected by John Foster (1993), 'Two Tankas', 'Fruit Picking', 'Giant' and 'A Bald-headed Man from Dundee', by permission of the author; **Gareth Owen**, 'Conversation Piece' and 'Den to Let' from *Collected Poems*, Macmillan Children's Books. Copyright © Gareth Owen, 2000, by permission of Rogers, Coleridge & White Ltd on behalf of the author; **Brian Patten**, 'Dear Mum' from *Thawing Frozen Frogs* by Brian Patten (1990) Viking. Copyright © Brian Patten 1990, 'The Mud Mother' and 'Jack Frost is Playing Cards at the Roadside' from *Juggling with Gerbils* by Brian Patten, Puffin Books (2000). Copyright © Brian Patten 2000, by permission of Rogers, Coleridge and White on behalf of the author, and 'Burying the Dog in the Garden' from *Gargling with Jelly*, Viking (1985), pp. 18-19. Copyright © Brian Patten, 1985, by permission of Penguin UK; **Jo Peters**, 'Seasons', 'The Seaside', 'My Hands' and 'What Am I?', by permission of the author; **Gervase Phinn**, 'Three Cinquains' and 'A Monster Alphabet', by permission of the author; **Simon Pitt**, 'At the End of School Assembly', first published in *The Bees Sneeze*, ed. G Boswell, Stride (1992), by permission of the author; **Sylvia Plath**, 'You're' from *Collected Poems* by Sylvia Plath, by permission of Faber & Faber Ltd; **Christine Potter**, 'Crocodile', by permission of the author; **John Pudney**, 'For Johnny' from *For Johnny*, Shepherd Walwyn, by permission of David Higham Associates on behalf of the author; **Irene Rawnsley**, 'True Confession', first published in *Fun with Poems*, Brilliant Publications (2000), 'The Caterpillar Fair', first published in *BBC Poetry Corner* (1993), and 'Sounds', by permission of the author; **Rita Ray**, 'And It's A . . .', by permission of the author; **John Rice**, 'Leisure Centre, Pleasure Centre' and 'Ettykett' from *Rockets & Quasars*, Aten Press (1984) and 'A Minute to Midnight', first published in *Read Me 2*, Macmillan Children's Books (1999), by permission of the author; **E. V. Rieu**, 'Cat's Funeral', by permission of Authors' Licensing & Collecting Society on behalf of the Estate of the author; **Michael Rosen**, 'Me and My Brother' from *One of Your Legs is Both the Same*, Macmillan Children's Books, 'From A Problem Page', 'Register' and 'Conversation' from *Wouldn't You Like to Know*, Andre Deutsch, and 'You Tell Me' from *You Tell Me*. Copyright © Michael Rosen, by permission of Peters Fraser and Dunlop Group Ltd on behalf of the author; **Coral Rumble**, 'Butterfly Inside', first published in *Sugar Cake Bubble*, ed. Brian Moses, Ginn (1999), 'Red' from *Creatures, Teachers and Family Features* by Coral Rumble, Macdonald Young Books (1999), 'Cats Can', 'My Team' and 'Guess Who?', by permission of the author; **Anita Marie Sackett**, 'Conkers' and 'Estuary', by permission of the author; **Vernon Scannell**, 'The Apple Raid' from *The Apple Raid*, Chatto & Windus (1974), 'Morning Meeting' and 'Epitaph for a Gifted Man', by permission of the author; **Fred Sedgwick**, 'Cinquain – Prayer, February Night', by permission of the author; **Andrea Shavick**, 'Hanukka' and 'Little Miss Muffet', first published in *Rhymes Around the Year*, Oxford University Press (2000), by permission of the author; **Matt Simpson**, 'Kicking Up

Acknowledgements

Leaves' and 'On-side Cinquain', by permission of the author; **Ian Souter**, 'My Dad is Amazing', by permission of the author; **Roger Stevens**, 'Poem for Sale', 'Louder', 'Policeman Haiku', 'Lowku Haiku', 'Smelly People', 'Julius Caesar', 'Michael Owen', 'Eight Swords', 'My Thin Friend', 'The You Can ABC' and 'Egyptian Afterlife', by permission of the author; **SuAndi**, 'Everybody Rap', by permission of the author; **Matthew Sweeney**, 'Down the River' from *The Flying Spring Onion* by Matthew Sweeney, by permission of Faber and Faber Ltd; **Marian Swinger**, 'Three Little Pigs', 'The Witches' School Of Flying' and 'An Intrepid Young Woman From Stock', by permission of the author; **Dylan Thomas**, 'The Song of the Mischievous Dog' from *Collected Poems*, J M Dent, by permission of David Higham Associates on behalf of the Estate of the author; **Nick Toczek**, 'Three Relatively Silly Poems', 'How the Bumble Bee Got His Stripes', 'Victorian Diarist', 'Riddle 1', 'Riddle 2', 'Crusher' and 'The Dragon Who Ate Our School', by permission of the author; **Shirley Tomlinson**, 'The Evacuee', by permission of the author; **Angela Topping**, 'Bumble-bee' and 'Yo Yo', by permission of the author; **Jill Townsend**, 'Tortoise And Hare Race', 'When Leaves Pile Up' and 'Letter To My Uncle', by permission of the author; **Jaroslav Vrchlicky**, 'For a Little Love', first published in *Sheep Don't Go To School*, ed. Andrew Fusek Peters, translated by Andrew and Vera Fusek Peters, Bloodaxe Books (1999), by permission of Andrew Fusek Peters; **Dave Ward**, 'Run, Run!', 'Bottles', 'Maggie and the Dinosaur' and 'We Want To Wear Our Wellies', by permission of the author; **Celia Warren**, 'Sounds Like Magic', first published in *Senses Poems*, ed. John Foster, Oxford University Press (1996), 'Football Training', first published in *They Think It's All Over*, Macmillan Children's Books (1998), 'Squirrel' from *Animals*, Reading 360, Ginn (1993), 'Penguins on Ice', first published in *Wacky Wild Animals*, ed. Brian Moses, Macmillan Children's Books (2000). 'As Tasty as a Picnic' and 'The Fox and the Grapes', by permission of the author; **Clive Webster**, 'See Me Walking', first published in *First Verses*, ed. John Foster, Oxford University Press (1996), by permission of the author; **Colin West**, 'An Alphabet of Horrible Habits', 'Toboggan' and 'Socks' from *The Best of West* by Colin West, Hutchinson (1990), by permission of the author; **Kit Wright**, 'March Dusk' from *Cat Among the Pigeons*, Viking (1987), p. 24. Copyright © Kit Wright 1984, by permission of Penguin UK; **Bernard Young**, 'Best Friends', 'Absent', 'Career Opportunity: Knight Required' and 'Birds of a Feather', by permission of the author; **Benjamin Zephaniah**, 'Remembrance Days', 'Vegan Delight' and 'A Day in the Life of Danny the Cat' from *Talking Turkeys* by Benjamin Zephaniah, Viking (1994), pp. 86, 30-31, 36-38. Copyright © Benjamin Zephaniah, 1994, and 'Pencil Me In' from *Funky Chickens*, Viking (1996), pp. 88-89. Copyright © Benjamin Zephaniah, 1996, by permission of Penguin UK.

Every effort has been made to trace the copyright holders but if any have been inadvertently overlooked the publishers will be pleased to make the necessary arrangement at the first opportunity.

Unzip Your Lips

100 Poems to Read Aloud chosen by Paul Cookson

100 poems to read aloud by 100 of the best modern poets from Causley to Moses to Patten.

Out in the Desert

Out in the desert lies the sphinx
It never eats and it never drinks
Its body quite solid without any chinks
And when the sky's all purples and pinx
(As if it was painted with coloured inx)
And the sun it ever so swiftly sinx
Behind the hills in a couple of twinx
You may hear (if you're lucky) a bell that clinx
And also tolls and also tinx
And they say at the very same sound the sphinx
It sometimes smiles and it sometimes winx.

But nobody knows just what it thinx.

Charles Causley

Read Me

A Poem for Every Day of the Year

READ ME contains a poems for every day of the year from the very best classic and modern poets.

Praise for READ ME

"This book contains Emily Dickinson, Wordsworth, Gareth Owen, Ian McMillan, Wes Magee, William Blake and Seamus Heaney – an excellent acknowledgement of the fact that some days we feel wordy and broody, and on other days we feel as brash as the wind, and no deeper than the surface of our skins. This anthology shows some respect for those changeable habits."

Michael Glover, Independent on Sunday

"Great riches are to be found between the covers of this unassuming paperback . . . this treasure trove celebrates the variety of English verse."

Beverley Davies, The Lady

"The poetic calendar chosen by Gaby Morgan is a delight: motley, wide-ranging and unpatronising."

Observer

Join In or Else

Poems for Joining In with chosen by Nick Toczek

A fantastic collection of poems to join in with, recite in class, say aloud with friends or even read on your own.

I Wrote Me a Poem

I wrote me some words and the words pleased me.
I told my words to the big oak tree.
My words went: "Jibber-jabber".
My song went: "Tree Shanty".
My limerick went: "Silly-billy".
My rhyme went: "Sky high".
My haiku went: "Slooooow thought."
My verse went: "Tickety-boo, tickety-boo".
My epic went: "Too long, much too long".
My ode went: "Lah . . . dah".
My sonnet went: "Oooh, love!"
My poem went: "Fiddle-eye-dee".

Bruce Barnes

A selected list of poetry books available from Macmillan

The prices shown below are correct at the time of going to press. However, Macmillan Publishers reserve the right to show new retail prices on covers which may differ from those previously advertised.

All Macmillan titles can be ordered at your local bookshop or are available by post from:

Book Service by Post
PO Box 29, Douglas, Isle of Man IM99 1BQ

Credit cards accepted. For details:
Telephone: 01624 675137
Fax: 01624 670923
E-mail: bookshop@enterprise.net

Free postage and packing in the UK.
Overseas customers: add £1 per book (paperback) and £3 per book (hardback).